Unequaled

How social justice, critical race theory, and the hunt for **equality** is destroying America and the Christian Church.

by Forrest Maready

**FEELS
LIKE
FIRE!**

Also by Forrest Maready:

Red Pill Gospel: Christianity, before it was ruined by Christians, 2020
The Autism Vaccine: The Story of Modern Medicine's Greatest Tragedy, 2019
The Moth in the Iron Lung: A Biography of Polio, 2018
Crooked:Man-made Disease Explained, 2018
Unvaccinated, 2018
Massa Damnata, 2017

**FEELS
LIKE
FIRE!**

Text copyright ©2020 by Forrest Maready
Cover Illustrations and Typography ©2020 by Forrest Maready
Printed in the United States of America

ISBN 979-8683794910
Library of Congress Control Number: 2020917899

Library of Congress Cataloging-in-Publication Data
Names: Maready, Forrest, author.
Title: Unequaled.
Subtitle: How social justice, critical race theory, and the hunt for equality is destroying America and the Christian Church.
Description: Wilmington, North Carolina : Feels Like Fire, [2020].
Identifiers: Library of Congress Control Number: 2020917899 (paperback) | ISBN: 979-8683794910 (paperback) Subjects: LCSH: POLITICS / Political Science | Philosophy. | RELIGION / Christian Theology / Apologetics.

Peace takes two. War, only one.

Strange Times

Throughout the world, at nearly any political, educational, or institutional organization, you are likely to find a large slice of their budget dedicated to a type of job which did not exist just a decade ago. With lofty titles like "Chief Diversity Officer" or "Equity Investigator," people are employed to ensure their organizations have made every effort to handle things fairly. In order that no one is discriminated against, these people are supposed to enact policies and procedures to give everyone—no matter their ability or intellect—an honest chance at excelling.

For instance, it might be the job of the "Director of Inclusive Leadership" to make certain those in charge of organizational matters reflect the opinions, genders, and skin tones of everyone they lead. The *Equity Investigator* might follow-up with surveys and phone calls and report back to the *Chief Diversity Officer* if irregularities are detected. Just twenty years ago, these offices, titles, and the educational fields of study which support them were nearly non-existent. Some within human resources might have managed an *affirmative action* program or monitored sexual harassment and discrimination initiatives, but there was nothing like the ten- and twenty-person offices that populate many organizations today.

As these new positions have been created, other changes have taken place which, at first, may seem unrelated. For instance, because there are people who prefer not to be referred to by traditional male or female labels—like "he" and "she" or "his" and "hers"—some places have essentially made it a potential criminal offense to refer to someone by the wrong gender pronoun. At universities, females are being allowed more time to finish certain exams than their male counterparts and in the military, physical tests are altered to ensure a more even gender distribution of successful applicants.

In England, police are raiding homes, busting in doors to arrest those convicted of "hate speech," a term which means vastly different things to anyone who has attempted to define it. Within the United States, military-style SWAT teams might raid someone's house and forcibly kidnap children because their parents refused a medical procedure the local health department insisted was necessary. Billionaire philanthropists are donating huge sums of money throughout the world on things like "environmental justice" and "gender equity." Even kindergartners are being taught about "bias" and "social justice."

Throughout the world, this singular focus on fairness has reached a fever-pitch and is easily visible in nearly every facet of our lives. For the millions of people who want nothing more than to level the playing field, there is one thing they will point towards as the cause of nearly all of the suffering in the world: *inequality*. Under their current thinking, there are numerous power structures in place that afford some people distinct advantages compared to others. It could be based on their ethnicity, their gender, their sexual identity, even their religion—but whatever it is, certain human attributes provide others with a superior starting position in each and every race they run. Those that benefit from these advantages need not even be aware of them to make use of them. They are simply there and nearly impossible—without the aid of those who make a living studying this kind of thing—to fairly compensate for.

Such people believe the effects of this imbalance to be systemic inequality that favors a few while disadvantaging others—an unfortunate reality responsible for nearly every social, economic, political, environmental, scientific, educational, and health woe in the world. This belief that many people are suffering because of the actions—or inaction—of a few can make its way into nearly any debate or conflict. Across the globe, any given weekend might feature massive protests regarding a number of complaints —many of which are suspected to be caused by this underlying disparity.

As a result, many have come to believe that if any endeavor be worth undertaking, jettisoning inequality from the book of human history could right a thousand wrongs. Indeed, our desire for equality burns so strongly we give awards to anyone for anything just for the appearance of reducing the sensation of unfairness. Caitlyn (Bruce) Jenner was given several honors, including Glamour magazine's *Woman of the Year* and ESPN's *Arthur Ashe Courage Award* simply for going public with his/her gender dysphoria and transition. United States President Barack Obama had barely spent a year in the White House before Norwegians awarded him the *Nobel Peace Prize*, an honor given not for any actual diplomacy he'd accomplished but instead as a result of their exuberant response to a bi-racial human being named to an esteemed political office.

The outpouring of support for those seen as overcoming adversity is so intense many people have purposefully taken on personas of those seen as suffering from inequality, a sociological *Munchausen syndrome by proxy*. Rachel Dolezal and Shaun King, who are either entirely—

or nearly entirely—Caucasian, have become famous making every attempt to portray themselves as African-Americans, the dedication to their appointed ethnicity evident in their work for the NAACP and Black Lives Matter movements. Elizabeth Warren, a politician who evidently grew up believing she was part-Indian, often leveraged this perceived slight for academic and employment advantages despite her lily-white appearance and aw-shucks persona.

The fanatical devotion to impartiality is pervasive and has extended well beyond academic campuses and government think tanks. Even corporate board meetings or informal conversations between friends will often feature ideas about how to solve the rampant inequality in the world. As more universities, corporations, and government agencies direct an increasing amount of resources towards achieving equality, the pressure on those who have made utopian promises of social and economic nirvana has continued to rise. *Compliance officers* and *equity investigators* are conducting more surveys and holding more conferences in an attempt to identify any remaining bias or unrecognized entitlement. The ominous presence of legal counsel and even law enforcement is more clearly visible—the unfortunate result of too many people enjoying too much of their unintended privilege. With an intense commitment to this belief, it's not hard to see how, for many, violence appears but a small price to pay for the promise of equality.

Given the backdrop of the religious wars of the past, it does not bode well that there is another group of people who feel very differently. They may find themselves at odds with those who strive for equality on nearly every political or social issue but are often unable to clearly articulate why. I was one of these people. I consistently ended up on the same side of many seemingly unrelated debates—consistent because I nearly always occupied the opposite side as those who fought so zealously for "diversity" and "inclusion."

Eventually, I began to ask some difficult questions that would force me to rethink this whole debate: What if inequality was intentional? What if inequality was created by God—on purpose? What if it was a key feature of the intricate machine of creation that allows each living thing to play a special role? What if the design of creation *requires* that we perform these roles? What if our refusal to accept this design is what is causing so much strife and conflict in the world? What if our rebellion against inequality is actually the root of all sin, the very thing that is breaking the natural order of God's creation right now?

Rot

Today, many of the treasured institutions that have made America a great place to live are being destroyed. We may not worry about drought or famine but other concerns keep many awake at night: Riots fill the streets as cities burn. Churches sit empty. Families and marriage are no longer held in high esteem. Social trust has disappeared. Public education is in shambles. Law and order are no longer respected. Nothing would appear safe from disruption as even something as obvious as the concept of what it means to be male or female is being upended.

Ominous signs of conflict surround us. Frayed nerves. Awkward conversations at family events. People losing their jobs for saying the wrong things. Others losing their bank accounts or the ability to conduct business simply for crossing the wrong people. For those brave enough to speak their mind, threats of harm and physical violence often await them. The decay has gone beyond losing the right to life, liberty, and the pursuit of happiness—the peace and prosperity of America we have enjoyed for most of our lives seems to be fading away.

The rot has begun to affect the Church as well. For those of us who practice Christianity, our beliefs are frequently the target of ridicule and derision, often pointed to as the blame for all the world's ills. What's worse—many Christians have themselves been caught unawares, swept up in their attempts to not offend or exclude. They have even begun to persecute their own brothers and sisters in Christ, insisting that—like their worldly comrades—the Gospel should not upset or disregard anyone, no matter the transgression.

Every day another church closes. Another pastor recants their faith. Another denomination folds to the demands of the world. Christianity is under serious attack, but most who attend worship services on Sunday morning are unaware of the epic battle playing out in Bible studies, congregations, and denominations throughout our country. Pastors are oblivious to what's happening or are unable—or unwilling—to guard our great faith. Congregants who have some inclination to defend the Gospel are left with nothing but a scripture reference to whisper to a screaming mob. If something does not change, we will soon be in danger of losing our ability to worship at all without persecution.

The blessings of America—our freedoms, our prosperity, and our ability to worship freely—were once sustained by a people united on many different fronts. Our culture, traditions, and ideals, enjoined by a unified walk with Christ, once formed a protective layer around those precious scriptures which inform our faith. Today is different. We are no longer united and are in grave danger of losing everything. The cultural shroud that gave weight to those scriptures is gone, and many have forgotten why they even exist. To them, many parts of the Bible sound like empty appeals from a bygone era.

Different groups have recently come together, a seemingly infinite variety of grievances marching through streets—shouting, spitting, looting, and burning their way across America and many other countries throughout the world. Their demands? A list which ranges from "racial justice" to the abolition of fossil fuels. Where are these attacks coming from? What is it that threatens our faith and nation so gravely? Some might say communism, socialism, or other variants of Marxist political and economic thought. Others might say it is critical race theory or identity politics—both of which seek to classify and rank people based on their skin color or perceived oppression.

While many factors affect these demonstrations, a quick look at a few events that have taken place over the last 150 years may provide us with some clues to help understand what is going on. The hundreds of groups and affiliations you might find marching or protesting on any given weekend may be reacting to the exact same grievance that's destroying Christian churches at breakneck speed. As it turns out, the motivations and aggravations which have led us to this point may not be so complex at all.

Social Justice

Before we take a closer look at specifically what is destroying America—and Christian churches throughout our land—we should spend a bit of time defining these concepts which, if properly addressed, are supposed to cure us of all the world's problems. Terms such as *social justice* and *critical race theory* have been around a while, but like many things associated with the progressive left, their definitions are fluid and constantly changing. Because of that, I'd like to define these things as I currently understand them.

Social justice is a term many people throw around casually—a universal good that any human on the planet ought to be fighting for. The bare-naked word "justice" typically referred to matters of law and order. If your family member was murdered, it would be natural for you to want justice—that is, the killer to be found and punished. If another family member was *wrongly* convicted of murder, you would also want justice for them—for them to be freed from a prison sentence that was mistakenly placed upon them.

Upholding justice is one of the most important things government can do—particularly when it's applied evenly. "Equal justice under the law," a key component of American civic life, is designed to guarantee fairness. For much of human history, those in government positions or a higher economic status could get away with breaking the law in ways that normal citizens could not. This imbalance inevitably led to violent revolts as lower class subjects reacted to being treated unfairly.

Because of this, the framers of America went to great pains to ensure that everyone—no matter their race, economic status, or political views—would be held to the same standard as everyone else. Obviously nothing is perfect, and it would seem that many in our nation's capital to be capable of all manner of transgression without so much as a single night in jail. Regardless, the intent to treat all American citizens equally under the law is crucial to political and social stability. If enough people sense they are not being treated fairly, violent upheaval is inevitable.

Social justice has taken this quest for fairness beyond the domain of criminal activity and into the realm of everyday life. It proposes that it is not enough for government to ensure equal treatment for those that break the law.

Instead, it supposes that the role of government is to make sure no one attends a better school than anyone else, lives in a nicer house than their neighbor, or even gets paid more than their coworkers. In short, it is the government's job to ensure each and every citizen *enjoys their life* as much as others do.

This is, of course, an impossible task, but it gets worse—social justice is not just concerned with equality, but *blame*. It suggests that for some to be poor while others are not is the result of oppression or other purposeful manipulation, rather than the result of one's own actions or perhaps, a stroke of luck. Because of this, fighting for social justice requires the cultivation of *envy* and the projection of imaginary crimes on those who are already *enjoying their lives*. Within the distortion of social justice, there is no standard of living high enough to be satisfied with if there are others living higher. And so government is tasked with something far beyond criminal or legal justice—the role of ensuring that everyone is equally content, a problem for which there is no solution.

While it originally focused on matters of economic status, housing, and schooling, social justice has grown to encompass many other areas. "Racial justice" is now being used to describe the activism undertaken to ensure particular races or ethnicities are enjoying their lives as much as others. "Gender justice" has taken on perceived unfairness between genders, be it job opportunities, social privileges, or anything else that might differentiate the sexes.

"Environmental justice" is a movement which has merged the goals of global-warming advocates with social justice activists. The poor and oppressed typically live in squalid areas of the world where health concerns from pollution and manufacturing waste are increased. Environmental justice activists seek to protect these people from harm and ensure they have access to living conditions that promote the same health and wellbeing as those who reside in more privileged areas of the world.

There are probably many other social justice spinoffs, with more to come, but suffice it to say, their numbers are growing. As a result, "justice"—as a standalone term—has begun to mean something entirely different than what you might think. Justice has come to mean equal *outcomes*. In the past, well-intentioned American citizens might have worked hard to ensure "equal opportunity" for all. If you've ever looked for a job, you will no doubt recall the paragraph or two nearly every company includes emphasizing how they won't discriminate on the basis of age, gender, race, or a hundred other attributes.

Despite decades of providing equal opportunities, there remain groups of people who don't have as much as others. Because of this, those who fight for "justice" have turned their focus towards equal outcomes rather than equal *opportunity*. When you hear protestors shouting, "No justice, no peace," this doesn't refer to criminals being punished more fairly and in fact, doesn't refer to criminals at all. Justice, in that context, means a time when and where everyone has as much stuff as everyone else. The second half of the saying, "no peace," is not so much a prediction that violence is likely until that time of "justice," but instead a warning of the techniques they will use to achieve it.

Just as "justice" has become a catch-all term used to describe an even distribution of wealth and power, "equity" has taken on new life. Equity is a term you'll hear mentioned often these days—gender equity, racial equity, and many others. Equity represents a transition from working for equal opportunity to equal outcome instead. Equality indicates an attempt at equal opportunity. Because this has clearly not worked to achieve "justice," organizations now work for equity—equal outcomes—instead of equality. If you see the word equity in your workplace or church, it should raise the bright red flag of alarm—it is used to indicate that nothing will be considered off limits to achieve their goal, no matter how draconian the measures may seem.

Finally, you will frequently hear the term "hate" lobbed at people. Hate is simply a word they use to describe someone who doesn't agree with them. It is a meaningless transposition of what used to indicate intense dislike but it's meaning has been so badly butchered, it isn't even worth trying to correct. Just understand what someone means if they accuse you of hate—you disagree with them, and that hurts. If someone has a sign in their front yard that reads, "Hate has no home here," just know that means if you don't agree with them, you are not welcome there.

Critical Race Theory

A quick word about something before we move on to critical race theory. You have likely heard the term "identity politics" being mentioned. Identity politics is a strange expression in that its definition is generally agreed upon by both the left, who find it laudable, and the right, who find it offensive. Identity politics generally supposes that your political views are shaped by the specifics of who you are (or who you identify yourself as). This sounds inoffensive, even mundane, at first blush. Whose politics wouldn't be shaped by who they are?

The identities of identity politics could be race, gender, religion, or nearly any other attribute. The problem occurs as people get grouped and categorized by these identities and the politics that are associated with them. Individual thought and beliefs can be consumed by the groups to which they belong. This is likely what led 2020 Presidential candidate Joe Biden to say to his African-American interviewer, "if you have a problem figuring out whether you're for me or Trump, then you ain't black."

Karl Marx, famous for proposing that all hostility could be attributed to the struggle between different economic classes, had nothing compared to this. For those on the left, identity politics provides a framework from which they can project oppression and foment envy through a seemingly infinite variety of grievances. More envy creates a greater desire for equity and justice—something the left revels in working to amend.

For many on the right, who view each person as an individual capable of their own thoughts and achievements, being grouped by these external categories is offensive. Just because someone is black doesn't mean they're for affirmative action. Just because someone is transgender doesn't require that they support non-biological females participating in female athletics. This isn't a simple rejection of stereotypes but something much larger—the respect for the individual over any collective group for which they are a part. Purposefully pitting various groups of people against each other has never been a hallmark of leaders of peaceful civilizations but that is just what many on the left are doing—whether they realize it or not.

Just so you're familiar with it, *intersectionality* is a useless term that simply describes the collection of these identities to which you belong—the overlap of the various groups which make you unique. This fancy word serves no purpose other than to stroke the egos of those who make their living causing division and strife with flowery language meant to confuse. Replace intersectionality with "uniqueness" and feel free to move on to contemplate something more worthwhile.

You may treat the term *inclusive* similarly. An inclusive organization simply means that, based on race, ethnicity, sexual orientation, or a thousand other measurements, it has a more even distribution of members. It doesn't matter that many females just don't like programming—the high school computer science club isn't inclusive until there are an even number of boys and girls. While this definition generally holds true, you should understand that inclusivity works in only one direction. An all-black football team could be considered to be fully inclusive. Similarly, an all-female editorial board at Huffington Post isn't in danger of being un-inclusive. Like *diversity*, inclusion often ends up meaning *less white males*.

What about *critical race theory*, a term that is increasingly being used throughout our country? Despite its fancy-sounding name, critical race theory is simply a race-specific version of identity politics—it proposes that rather than ignoring the color of someone's skin, we obsess over it. In critical race theory, *everything* can be attributed to the color of your skin, likely the sole reason you are either content with your life or oppressed and unhappy.

Like many schools of progressive thought, definitions change by the day, but in general, critical race theory focuses on the relationship between whites and blacks. It proposes that whites are racist simply because of their skin color. It proposes that blacks are oppressed simply because of their skin color. It doesn't matter whether you *feel* racist or not, you have unwittingly committed acts of racism because you are white. Even the most successful billionaire can suffer the effects of oppression, provided they are black.

In the same way justice and equity have taken on new meanings, so too has the term "racism." Under the influence of critical race theory, racism no longer means purposefully penalizing or mistreating someone because of their race or ethnicity—it indicates a state of unfairness, specifically between caucasians and "people of color." If you drive a nicer car than your neighbor, and you are white and they are not, that means you are "racist." It is not about the respect you show others. It is not about equal treatment you provide. Even if you have hired less qualified candidates under the guise of "affirmative action" within your small business at great cost to productivity, if you take home a bigger paycheck than your employees, you are racist.

This thinking has led racism to become the supposed cause of any inequality between certain people groups. How this hopeless trap is supposed to make your life better is anyone's guess. Regardless, it has worked its way into nearly every facet of public and private life. Social justice initially focused on government legislation to right the injustices it perceived but as calls for "justice" and discussions around critical race theory have become more ubiquitous, the indoctrination of their ideals has spread.

Corporate CEOs and HR officers send out dreaded "Diversity and Inclusion" emails, with calls to their employees to blot out racism from within their ranks through indoctrination within ominously-titled "Business Resource Groups." Entire government divisions such as the Department of Homeland Security and the National Credit Union Administration have fallen prey and have implemented mandatory diversity training programs. Sandia National Laboratories, which produces America's nuclear weapons, recently held a multi-day workshop specifically for its white employees, where they were asked to write letters of apology for their racism.

Nowhere has the wake of such destruction been felt more keenly than in churches across America, where pastors and their congregations are wholly unprepared to face screams of "racism" if they raise even the slightest objection to this madness. In 2019, the Southern Baptist Convention, recently a bulwark of conservative thought within Christian America, voted to include critical race theory as "an analytical tool" within their organization—a tepid endorsement meant to temper the objections of those who can see the darkness towards which we are headed. A growing number of astute churches have already left the denomination as they realize it's likely only a matter of time before the organization has been completely taken over.

Other churches host inter-denomination and inter-faith services in an attempt to assuage the guilt that is being foist upon them, with racial reconciliation a frequent theme. As Father Kenneth Boller of St. Francis Xavier Catholic Church in New York City recently intoned to his congregation during a regular Sunday service, "Do you affirm that white privilege and the culture of white supremacy must be dismantled where it is present? Do you support racial equity, racial justice, and liberation for every person?"

"Yes," the parishioners responded, convinced they were guilty of sin they had not committed, the portraits of George Floyd, Ahmaud Arbery, and Breonna Taylor—three black people thought to have been killed due to the racism of white people—taking the place of wine and bread on the Communion table. With the inexorable creep of critical race theory well within its walls, Southern Baptist churches will likely soon find their congregations hating America, praying not for souls to be saved or God's kingdom to be advanced, but instead for justice and equity. As has happened with many other churches before them, it is likely they will eventually come to hate the Gospel story itself and will reference Jesus not as Savior but simply a man of great charity.

Danger

To suggest that social justice and critical race theory have taken the place of Christianity in many American's hearts can not be considered controversial at this point. Their sermons reflect it. Their songs reflect it. Even their prayers reflect it—confessions and vows recited for each other's approval rather than God above.

But it is not just the Christian church that is in danger. Many of the leaders of these movements are openly calling for an end to our country. No longer content to "be the change you want to see," proponents of social justice and critical race theory are leading classes and workshops throughout denominations and government organizations where "death to America," is a central theme.

Recently, an organization funded by the Department of Education, held a conference on "abolishing the United States." Keynote speaker Bettina Love opened the affair by announcing that the United States had oppressed people of color for over 400 years and that only by tearing the system down could these wrongs be made right. Quoting from authors Stefano Harvey and Fred Moten's *The Undercommons: Fugitive Planning and Black Study,* Love insisted the abolition of America was "not so much the abolition of prisons but the abolition of a society that could have prisons, that could have slavery, that could have the wage, and therefore not abolition as the elimination of anything but abolition as the founding of a new society."

America is not without its faults, of course, and there is much that can be improved upon. But to suggest that it needs to be "abolished," because of the way it has treated certain races is laughable. Our nation is the destination of choice for millions of immigrants from around the world— of every race and ethnicity—specifically for our *lack* of racism, not an abundance of it. Even the use of the term "abolish" might be considered offensive, given the hundreds of thousands of Americans who died amidst fighting that played a large part in ending slavery within the United States.

There is one final mockery many of those who traffic in social justice and critical race theory often commit, one that should concern anyone paying attention. In addition to their desire for the abolition of the United States, they often call for the abolition of another group—a group they claim is responsible for all of the world's woes.

"We must abolish whiteness," one of them might whisper, their stifled tone meant for dramatic effect rather than stealth or secrecy. "Mute White People," a recent filter in Facebook's popular Instagram social media app was called, a feature which allowed their users to easily make their racial preferences known on their photos. One might assume these statements to be hyperbole, the angry outburst of a recent college graduate or angst-ridden teen designed to generate clicks. But these sorts of statements are routinely issued by intelligent professionals within the highest levels of government and corporate America. Teachers have been particularly affected, often attending rallies and protests where how to end "whiteness" is often discussed—through bullhorns and private conversations.

In the past, newsmakers and talking heads would have feigned surprise at these sorts of declarations. More recently, as Black Lives Matter protestors rampage through streets, screaming "F*** White People" at elderly Americans dining in outdoor restaurants, these statements have become too numerous to even track—their shock-value completely gone. Throughout our land, the demise of our nation is routinely called for, and white people along with it.

Metaphor or not, the sheer volume and conviction of these statements should serve as a wakeup call to those who treasure the original ideals of our nation's founding, particularly the concept of equal justice under the law. Not only is the nation we call home under intense attack, an entire race (and gender) of people who took part in its creation is as well.

Amish 2.0

On our honeymoon, my wife and I were riding across Canada by train and happened to share our journey with a large Amish community traveling westward. One night we went to the dining car to eat but found it was full—except for a table in the back with a young Amish couple sitting by themselves. With two seats available and an insatiable curiosity, I approached them and asked if we could join them for dinner. They graciously accepted in broken English and we sat down for what I knew would be an unforgettable meal.

In Pennsylvania, Ohio, Indiana, and many other states, close-knit communities of Amish appear to live in a very distant time. They wear distinct clothing with clasps or pins instead of zippers or buttons, drive horses and buggies instead of cars, and go to great lengths to avoid many other modern conveniences we take for granted. Their customs and language might seem foreign, but for many of us twenty-first-century folk, there is a deep fascination with their willingness to forego contemporary inventions for a more simple way of life.

While most people associate the Amish with their humble farms and "Little House on the Prairie" attire, the pursuit of this unique agrarian lifestyle was not what originally made them distinct. Initially, they would have appeared similar to their neighbors, who also farmed animals and produce. Their tools and machines were just as advanced. It was something else that led them to immigrate to America in the 1700s, a deep split within the church that pitted Christian against Christian in fights—even wars—to the death.

As believers broke from the religious rule of the Catholic church, the ensuing political upheaval would claim hundreds of thousands of lives. The Amish emerged from a group of people called Anabaptists who thought people should be baptized once they had confessed their faith in Jesus. The prevailing notion was that only infants should be baptized and to insinuate this sacred rite was meaningless by conducting a second baptism did not go over well. This seemingly trivial difference in belief led to many people being killed in the most horrific ways possible—a list for which burning alive at the stake and live disembowelment only begin to enumerate. In order to escape the likelihood of death for their convictions, the Amish believers began to leave Europe for Pennsylvania and other parts of America.

Why would such a slight distinction cause so many people to feel that death for those who differed was a fitting punishment? It is a complex answer but a significant piece of the puzzle can be traced to the control of power. Both kings and popes were widely accepted as divinely chosen and their word was as good as God's law. For those in power, they depended on the religious devotion of their followers. To dispute prevailing religious dogma was to question their legitimacy. For kings and popes—who had not been chosen by the vote of common people—there was but a thin veneer of belief that separated their demise from an angry mob.

As many Christians began to question the power structures and corruption of the Catholic church, the papacy felt threatened and responded with brutality. Other political entities, whose religious doctrines defined them, joined in. Those who expressed a contrasting belief might be publicly hanged to near death, cut down and flayed alive on a wooden table, their body parts displayed around the city as a warning to others. Over the next few centuries, other Christian groups would temporarily supplant the Catholic church as the dominant player and would inflict equally barbaric punishment to those who did not "bend the knee" to their beliefs.

We seldom consider the reason for the separation of church and state in America but it was a crucial component of our founding documents—specifically because of the violence that stemmed from the religious power struggles of the day. Despite our often misguided understanding of it today, the partition was originally meant to protect warring Christians from each other, both of whom would use government power to enforce their beliefs, a practice which had created constant social and political instability.

It's important to understand the nature of the schism that first led the Amish to escape Europe because today we are in the opening stages of another—a deep rift that has cut our country, our world even, in half and threatens to turn deadly any moment. Nearly everyone can sense the ominous clouds that hang over our political and social discourse every day but are likely unable to put their finger on just what—and why—we are so angry.

As it turns out, there may be something very simple—a difference in a single core belief—that many of our most contentious disputes originate from. This disparity has been growing, percolating beneath the surface for over two hundred years and like a brood of long-hidden cicadas, it has finally begun to emerge, covering every thought and interaction with hostility and resentment. But unlike infant baptism or predestination arguments of old, this quarrel involves something much more contentious.

Heretics aren't being burned at the stakes—although it sometimes feels not far off. So before we descend into madness and the fog of war, a serious look at what this specific difference is—and how it came to exist—may serve to strengthen our resolve. As we sit restlessly in the growing shadow of conflict, it is my sincere hope—and prayer—these next few chapters provide you with clarity as to where things went wrong.

Diversity Or Equality

A misunderstanding of the nature of equality will prevent America or any other nation from ever having peace. Get this wrong—which we certainly have—and nothing else will work. Everything else will be unhappiness, chaos, violence, and death. Get this right and sustaining a nation that honors God and provides peace and stability for its people will be much easier. So how is this issue of equality dividing our nation—and world—in half?

You might think of there being two types of people in the world: Either you want the world to be full of equality, or you want the world to be full of diversity. You cannot have both. You must choose one or the other. Equality or diversity. The world is splitting apart right now as churches, races, and nations—groups that recently thought that they were unified—realize they are full of people with differing opinions about this issue. Where do you stand? What is it that you want? Equality? Or diversity?

Many people believe everyone in the world is equal to one another. Men are equal to women. Girls are equal to boys. Children are equal to adults. Asians are equal to Europeans and Whites are equal to Blacks. Everything is identical. No matter some obvious differences in physical appearance, just beneath the surface, everyone is the exact same—universally interchangeable, without any effect on the grand machine in which all play a part.

Does this sound like you? If it does, you're what is called an *egalitarian*. If you're an egalitarian, you believe that everyone is equal. You also likely believe that if there *are* any apparent differences—beyond physical appearance— these are *not* due to some genetic or intellectual difference between groups of people, but due to a system which has been built up over decades, if not centuries, to favor a particular group.

If you believe everyone is truly equal then take a few minutes to observe the world. You will, no doubt, notice that no matter where you look, things are *not* equal. This is true amongst animals, plants, and most certainly among humans. Some have plenty while others have less. Some live in countries bound by centuries of oppression, while others enjoy a life of relative freedom. How can this be? If in a natural state, everyone is truly equal, why doesn't the world reflect it? Unfortunately, a popular way to explain the inequality we see in the world is to suggest an unnatural event: Someone must have caused it. Some person or group of people acted in an unnatural way to upset the natural balance of equality in order to favor one group over the other.

If you don't feel like you're an egalitarian, you may find yourself more comfortable as what people call a *complementarian*. Complementarians admit that these groups—all of them, in fact—are very different. Women and men. Children and adults. Asians and Europeans. Blacks and Whites. They may complement each other sometimes, but not always. They're not universally interchangeable. Beyond superficial distinctions of physical appearance lie more profound differences.

Complementarians accept these differences as part of the natural order of life, clearly visible in the relationship between every connected plant, animal—even between geographical or meteorological phenomena. The complementarian believes that these differences are not a bug in the system but a feature. In other words, distinctions between men and women, children and adults, and even between races or ethnicities don't represent a flawed creation, but the essential design of a perfectly balanced machine, each element playing its proper role.

For most of human history, the complementarian viewpoint was unchallenged. It was considered obvious. Each gender had roles they were more suited for. Men hunted, women fed. Older people instructed, children listened and learned. Throughout the ebb and flow of life, these distinctions and responsibilities each group played were considered obvious and an enjoyable part of what defined one's existence. They were a crucial part of your identity. As author and theologian C. S. Lewis put it:

> *Equality (outside mathematics) is a purely social conception. It applies to man as a political and economic animal. It has no place in the world of the mind. Beauty is not democratic— she reveals herself more to the few than to the many, more to the persistent and disciplined seekers than to the careless. Virtue is not democratic—she is achieved by those who pursue her more hotly than most men. Truth is not democratic—she demands special talents and special industry in those to whom she gives her favors. Political democracy is doomed if it tries to extend its demand for equality into these higher spheres. Ethical, intellectual, or aesthetic democracy is death.*

In the last hundred years, the egalitarian concept has begun to dominate and is attempting to tear down the notion of gender, race, or any other kind of distinction. It insists that only when everything is equal can humans enjoy their lives. Whether it be child-rearing or money-earning, nursing an infant or fighting in wars, the notion that any living soul can successfully complete any of the other's tasks has become paramount to the egalitarian worldview. And it is causing many, many problems.

Distinctions

Egalitarians are often very compassionate people. They feel that anything less than perfect equality is unfair. Rather than accept the complex interplay of humanity, they seek to unify it—to remove all diversity and fashion everyone into identical, interchangeable pieces.

The other viewpoint—complementarians—are different. They are also compassionate people, but rather than trying to reshape the world into something they feel it was never intended to be, they celebrate each other's differences as beautiful distinctions that have sustained human life on this planet for ages. Take a moment and think about how you view the world. Would you consider yourself an egalitarian or a complementarian? It's important for you to understand the lens through which you view things.

These two different viewpoints form the basis of nearly every political and ideological distinction there is. No matter the argument, if you are an egalitarian, you will almost always find yourself siding with other egalitarians, be it the death penalty, abortion, affirmative action, open borders—the list goes on and on. Similarly, if you are a complementarian, you will often find yourself in agreement on seemingly unrelated political or social issues with other complementarians. This one viewpoint determines much about how you understand the world.

It is curious to note that both groups act out seemingly the opposite of what they profess to believe. Egalitarians consider everyone to be equal but push special advantages and disadvantages for certain groups. Affirmative action allows particular ethnicities to qualify for schooling or employment even though their qualifications may fall short. Progressive tax brackets penalize those who work hard and are too successful. Throughout the egalitarian mindset, they preach that everyone is equal then treat them as if they're not.

Complementarians accept that everyone is different, with varying abilities for physical activity, nurturing, academic pursuits, or leadership, but favor treating everyone the same—as if there were no distinctions. For example, everyone should have the same requirements for becoming a fire fighter. If you're a woman, you should still have to be able to carry a 160-pound sandbag up and down a ladder. If you're a black scientist or violin player, you should receive no special preference for being hired over a similarly qualified candidate.

Why this disparity? Why do egalitarians, who profess that everyone is equal, treat groups so differently? And why do complementarians, who freely admit that everyone is different, treat many things the same? The reason is obvious once you see it.

The actions of both groups serve the same purpose—to reinforce the world in the way they imagine it to exist. For the complementarian, treating everyone as if they are the same ensures that distinctions remain visible and obvious. If a woman cannot carry a 160-pound sandbag up and down the ladder, then perhaps she shouldn't be a firefighter after all. If a high school dropout cannot complete a basic math test, then perhaps a job as a calculus professor is not a good fit for him. But to put your thumb on the scale, so to speak, and place these people in roles they are not a good fit for, will certainly cause frustration and resentment for those who were told they were perfect for the job. Even worse, it may endanger the financial well-being or physical lives of others they come in contact with, no matter how noble your intentions in hiring them were.

Complementarians accept the world as sometimes favoring one group over another, full of distinctions at every turn. Through charity, mission work, or personal effort, the complementarian often does the work of helping those in the need. They don't believe inequality to be a temporary abnormality of creation that can be removed or permanently fixed. Instead, they acknowledge the diversity it creates and embrace the cooperation and dependence required to sustain human life because of it.

On the other end of the spectrum are egalitarians. They reject this kind of diversity as an essential, integral part of human existence. They seek to create an equal society, its diversity only as deep as the color of one's skin. In this society, men can menstruate or give birth, anyone can be a soldier or nuclear physicist, and children can govern—provided they have the correct ideology.

Egalitarians will spare no expense at re-shaping the world into a more equal state, facilitating the redistribution of wealth, knowledge, land, and power in their attempts. Even what might have once been thought of as un-fungible definitions—gender and ethnicity—are now allowed to be freely manipulated in order that a more "equitable" society exist.

Because egalitarians believe the fact that everything is *not* equal to be an unnatural state of affairs, it unfortunately follows that blame must be ascribed to explain its existence. Someone, or group of people, must be held accountable for bringing imbalance into the world. I'm talking, of course, about white privilege, the egalitarian's concept of original sin.

Equal, But Privileged

Much like the fall of Adam and Eve in the garden of Eden caused what could have been eternal separation from God, the egalitarian supposes the world lived in perfect equality until a particular race—and gender—of people were able to subvert the natural order and dominate others. This is what many now call *white privilege.*

While the complementarian might think of all ethnicities and genders as equal in the sight of God, the egalitarian places white males squarely at the bottom, forever guilty of supremacy and domination. Despite everyone being equal, the "privilege" mindset supposes that white males are cunning—or fortunate—enough to exploit all other ethnicities and genders. Despite believing everyone to be equal, egalitarians also insist that people of color are uniquely vulnerable to the oppression of white privilege.

What about the Declaration of Independence you might ask? What about the Bible? Doesn't it say all men are created equal? How could anyone say that one group is better than another? The equality the Declaration of Independence describes is much different than saying everyone is exactly the same. It describes a universal right of everyone to pursue personal liberty or happiness. It proscribes this as a universal right specifically *because* we are not equal in talent, intelligence, physical ability or any other measurement.

If we were all equal, this statement from the Declaration of Independence wouldn't even be necessary. Instead, it acknowledges these differences, in effect, by saying, "It doesn't matter how rich you are, how poor you are, how smart or dumb... Whether you're famous or completely unknown—*none* of that matters when it comes to *your* right to life, liberty, and the pursuit of happiness. Everyone, no matter who they are, gets these same rights." This statement in the Declaration of Independence *affirms* our differences more than anything.

And what about the Bible—doesn't it say God loves all of his creation equally? Yes, of course. I believe this. If you also believe this *but* insist that God made all of his creation into equal beings, despite the obvious distinctions that make life itself possible, you are rejecting the most essential reality of all—we are not equal to God. God is above us, holy, to be exalted. He has designed things as he, and not us, saw fit. We exist—each of us—as an integral and unique piece of the intricate puzzle he spoke into existence. But even so, we are all very different. We are not interchangeable. We all have a particular role to play, whether we like it or not. Husbands, wives, children—on and on the distinctions go.

Trying to govern a nation of people divided in half along this issue is nearly impossible. If you believe that if it wasn't for white privilege all of humanity would be able to live peacefully together, you are probably not going to enjoy living beside those who believe equality *never* existed to begin with.

I believe understanding the difference between these two viewpoints to be an essential component of understanding how we can move forward as humans in such a way to maximize peace and prosperity. I don't think there is any point in trying to reach a compromise on this issue. If you are an egalitarian and believe equality to be the highest, most noble calling of humanity, then you will never get along with someone who is a complementarian. You will always disagree on things. Complementarians believe equality doesn't exist anywhere naturally, has never existed anywhere—even artificially—and humans have only created more death and destruction over the past 200 years trying to force it into existence.

God's Design

Blood clotting is a miraculous component of nearly all living creatures. The blood that flows throughout the veins and arteries of our body serves many important functions. Among other things, it transports oxygen and carbon dioxide around the body and helps to ensure white blood cells are able to reach areas of infection or inflammation. Although our body is constantly creating new blood cells, we would live every day with the risk of a horrible death were it not for the ability of our blood to clot.

Internally or externally, the organs and vessels which ferry blood around our body can be damaged, an inevitable occurrence amongst the rough and tumble world. When this happens, the precious fluid that sustains life begins to leak. Normally, this opening would continue to drain blood until one were able to plug it up somehow, just like an old car tire. But God's design accounted for this and provides a natural method to heal.

Immediately after an injury, nearby blood vessels constrict in order to reduce the blood flow to that area. A chemical signal activates platelets to stick to the walls of the injured site—and each other—further slowing down the ability for blood to escape. Other proteins are signaled, creating long strands of what are called fibrin that get tangled within the platelets. A protective mesh is formed over the area, and eventually it grows dense enough that no additional blood can escape. Outside the body, blood cells cling together and form a protective surface over the injured tissue—what we could call a scab. Without this temporary layer of security, the body's immune system might struggle to defend against the intrusion of foreign microbes.

At this point, another miraculous event occurs—the body signals the whole sequence to stop. The platelets and fibrin have done their job, but without the ability of the body to recognize when just enough work has been done, the clotting signals would cascade throughout the body until the entire circulatory system turned into a giant clot —a similar effect to getting bitten by certain venomous snakes. Thankfully, this intricate system of blood-clotting normally works perfectly and after a skinned knee or scraped elbow, we don't put much thought into the remarkable sequence of events that spare someone a horrible death. Throughout the planet, this complex interplay between related components never ceases to amaze and although we haven't studied far beyond our solar system, it should not surprise us to see this theme continue infinitely.

In a perfect world, the distinctions between various groups of people would cause no resentment and everyone would readily accept their station in life as essential to a greater good. But as Adam and Eve ate from the Tree of Knowledge, the resulting cosmic realization gave birth to the first sin. Before then, they lived in perfect communion with God, blissfully unaware their hierarchical relationship with their creator would one day turn so many of their descendants against him. After they ate from the Tree of Knowledge, they need to have only realized a single thing for the fall of mankind to be complete—that God was God and they were not. That they were *unequal* to him. That they were but a part of a grander thing. That they occupied a rung on a ladder that placed them below God and in fact, were designed in such a way they *needed* God. For the first time in history, a human was humiliated. Not humbled, but humiliated.

If creation consisted of a single man or woman on a desert island—without the presence of God—sin would be essentially non-existent as there would be no *other* to sin against. By populating the earth at first with Adam, then Eve, God knowingly created the potential for sin. Yet still, in the Garden of Eden, sin did not initially exist. The earth's first two humans were unaware there was anything wrong with the pecking order through which creation would function. All it took was a bite from the Tree of Knowledge. All it took was a sliver of self-awareness—the seed of pride —for them to immediately regret that God was greater than they. The fact they noticed they were naked and wanted clothing to cover themselves was a trivial effect, a small price to pay compared to the more profound revelation of discovering that they were unequal.

This original sin did not introduce inequality into an egalitarian world, but simply caused Adam and Eve to begin to view the natural order of creation—humans below, with God on top—as offensive. They began to see what before had appeared perfect as an error in creation, something which needed to be remedied. The perfect communion of the garden was now seen as ruined and the arc of the Old Testament would soon begin to take shape. Their natural instincts of gratitude and thanksgiving had been tarnished and as a result, God began to command that his children worship him.

In the past, the church has withstood fearsome attacks. Atheists have attempted to prove God does not exist. Agnostics have attempted to prove the nature of his being is irrelevant. The church has stood strong and weathered these attacks. But over the last one hundred years, a significant evolution has happened. Through scientific and technological progress, our understanding of the inner-workings of humanity has improved the quality of life for humans everywhere. Unfortunately, it may have come at great cost.

Just as we are increasingly able to comprehend the complexity of Creation, we have begun to reject the notion that the template from which we were created requires different things to perform different roles. Clearly, this is a reality many are not comfortable with and now, rather than rebelling against God, they are focused on revolting against the natural order of creation itself. Inequality, no matter how slight or innocuous, is now seen as evil, something which must be destroyed, no matter the collateral damage.

The reason this new line of attack is so devastating is because Christians themselves have fallen for it. They have jumped ship and are unable—or unwilling—to defend the natural order. It's rare that a week will pass without reports of another church or denomination folding under the pressure of its own congregation to relinquish another long-held belief of Christendom. Indeed, many are knocking themselves over in attempts to assure those outside their church of their steadfast belief in equality, confident that Jesus would have capitulated similarly.

The fallout from this surrender now surrounds us. It envelopes us, yet we cannot see it. We nostalgically pine for the safety and security of days long gone but have no clue that we, ourselves, are the author of our own destruction. We shake our heads in disgust as other believers in the faith succumb to the pressure to conform, but offer little support to others who attempt to defend the Gospel.

It should then make sense to flesh out where and how we have gone wrong—where we strayed from God's natural order and attempted to replace the blueprint of creation with a man-made scheme. It is human nature to look away from things which make us uncomfortable, and many may have never seriously contemplated the cost of our rebellion. Because of that, I'm going to spend a short amount of time looking at a few obvious—and not so obvious—ways our insistence on equality has planted the seeds of devastation.

Jack and Jill

In the late 1800s, groups of women began to insist on something they previously never had: the right to vote in political elections. These "suffragettes," as they were called, formed organizations, held demonstrations, and printed tracts demanding that they be treated equally and allowed to cast their ballots like men. Standing in their way were much larger groups, equally vocal and just as committed to *preventing* the goal of women's suffrage. It may surprise you that these groups were also made up of women who campaigned tirelessly against the efforts of the suffragettes.

In 1913, a special bit of legislation—called the Drury bill —was put forth in Massachusetts that would have allowed women a chance to vote "Yes" or "No" on the issue of women's suffrage. The suffragists—those wanting women to be able to vote—worked hard *against* the bill specifically because they knew how pitiful their numbers would appear if an official count of the opinion of the majority of women was published. Nevertheless, over the next few years women's suffrage eventually gained the upper hand and what had been a state-by-state anomaly became nationwide law with the passing of the 19th Constitutional Amendment in 1919—a provision which prohibited state or federal restrictions for voting based on gender. Other countries enacted similar legislation around this same time period, the results of which are widely considered to be one of the most important leaps forward in the history of Civil Rights.

It is interesting to read through essays—penned by women—in that era in an attempt to glean why the majority of them were fighting *against* their right to vote. One of the most common complaints mentioned their unfamiliarity with the political world and their unlikelihood to spend enough time studying the issues and candidates to feel they could make wise decisions at the ballot box. Given the lackadaisical approach most take to voting today, their earnestness is refreshing. However, many offered another reason their vote was unnecessary: their husband was already voting on their behalf and creating an obligation for both of them to go to the ballot box was viewed as a gargantuan waste of time and resources.

Scattered throughout their writings is another theme impossible to miss: they just weren't interested. They had no desire to meddle with the "stressful affairs of men," just as they couldn't imagine men taking an interest in mending their children's clothes or cooking family dinners. Their domain of expertise was mostly unrelated to political affairs and where there was crossover, they were confident their husband's vote would reflect what they desired anyway.

The notion that a women's place is in the home may offend today, but less than a hundred years ago and for millenia that preceded, it was readily accepted by both men and women—a truth so obvious, so common, it wasn't even spoken of. Men handled the stressful affairs of setting public policy, forging alliances, and fighting wars and women steered as far away as they could. Raising children, nurturing their families, and easing the burden of trying to survive in an unforgiving world was hard enough as it was. The domains of women and men were clearly delineated, their roles defined, and it worked. The unique attributes of both genders were employed efficiently, the natural result of thousands of generations of trial and error.

As boys and girls grew up, they became familiar with their differences and enjoyed mimicking the adult roles they would undertake: girls, playing with dolls, changing their clothes, nurturing and instructing. Boys, playing with swords or guns, creating conflict, resolving it, climbing trees and developing courage and self-confidence. The female preference for human interaction and male preference for object/tool interaction is present from birth, but traditional custom held they should be reinforced anyway. And so they were, from mother to daughter and father to son. By the time a girl reached her teenage years, she was excited to put to use all that she had been taught as she yearned for a family of her own. Similarly, boys could not wait to prove their mettle in the world—to show their bravery, their ability to protect or defend, or to make their fathers proud.

With the introduction of the female vote, the transition of many civilized countries from what had been for thousands of years a patriarchal—or male-led—culture into a matriarchal society began. Its effects would soon surface. Long before government got involved, America had taken care of its poor effectively—an enterprise largely run by women. Once women acquired the ability to vote, they began to channel their nurturing instincts into empowering State enterprises rather than charity, clearly visible in the upward turn of graphs of government spending on social causes soon after 1919. Unfortunately, rather than helping anyone, the result of government welfare and public aid have been a catastrophic failure of charity or compassion, encouraging generations of fatherless children with a raging sense of entitlement.

Laws on immigration would soon be relaxed, the inevitable result of a populace more concerned with nurturing than protecting. This has lead to the madness of today where women—who have purposefully shunned marriage and children—scream for completely open borders, a plea for national suicide if there ever was one. Because appeals to defend our borders are being ridiculed in sufficient numbers, the natural instincts of men to protect that which they hold dear is smothered, a suppression one day we will pray to God to undo.

Around this same time, gender distinctions began to change—slowly at first, but accelerating over the next few decades. Initially, the differences seemed quaint. The bob haircuts and trousers of the 1920s and Sadie Hawkins dances of the 1930s were contentious at the time but may one day be seen as the odious beginning of the destruction this gender-bending rebellion has caused.

Today, we have domineering women who control their family's every decision, asserting authority—both emotionally and financially—over their husband and children. We have generations of effeminate men whose idea of protecting their family from harm is being able to dial 911 quickly or telling an intruder that he has no guns. As a result, children who grow up under this distorted model have little chance of a healthy marriage, themselves likely to replicate the perverted gender roles they are accustomed to.

Just a few generations of this madness have created the wicked world we now inhabit. Communities have lost respect for the police who serve them, their female officers unable to project power or authority over anyone. Law and order is being destroyed as ineffectual judges issue lenient sentences to immigrants who have raped and murdered, confident their compassion is enough to change the hearts of monsters.

Girls are constantly told they don't need boys for anything. Young men who, for their entire lifetimes, have been told all of the world's ills are largely due to their natural male instincts, lash out in epic fits of murderous rage and violence, killing as many people as they can before taking their own lives. Cross-dressing men, many with criminal records for assault and pedophilia, are featured at public library events to read books to children. Abortion-provider Planned Parenthood chapters host exotic pole-dancing parties for people of all ages. With the help of their doctors, misguided parents, convinced their children are the wrong gender, administer life-altering pharmaceuticals to 7-year-olds that may forever destroy their ability to have children.

From participation trophies to the banning of applause. From Mattel's gender-neutral toy line to private schools making boys and girls wear the exact same uniform. From demented feminists who paint with menstrual blood to womanish men who celebrate their wives' adultery. If you have shielded yourself from the sickening effects of our transition into a matriarchal society, they may come as a surprise to you. You might believe I have selected a few outrageous news articles for their shock value, but I can assure you, these sorts of events are constantly happening and there are far more wicked things I won't even discuss.

The end result has been the creation of enmity between man and woman, something the Serpent couldn't have dreamed of accomplishing in the Garden of Eden. Throughout the world, the consequences of our rebellion against the natural order of male and female surrounds us and, by itself, is fully capable of destroying our civilization. It should come as no surprise we have come to this place as, throughout the Old Testament, God warns us time and again we will be punished for disobeying him. And this time, we have certainly disobeyed—we have revolted against the very fabric of his creation.

Economy

From this bird's-eye view, the collapse our culture has suffered over the last one hundred years should make anyone reconsider the effects of attempting to inject equality where it does not exist. However, another battle with inequality has existed for much longer—one that has killed tens of millions of people.

Since the Greeks in 600 B.C., humans have attempted to temper the unpredictably of man to create a more equitable society. Various approaches to managing the government and economy were unsuccessfully tried, invariably a rebellion against what was thought to be abuse by a selfish dictator or monarch. It wasn't until the 1800s, as science and technology advanced beyond their wildest dreams, that many came to believe that economic and political progress would inevitably follow—progress most importantly employed in the dismantling of inequality.

Communism and its little sibling, socialism, made their appearance on the world stage with grandiose promises of a utopian society. Under various forms of these political models, it was hoped that everyone could receive an equal share and that no one would be left behind. With the introduction of these various forms of collectivism, humans began to take seriously their dreams of a better world.

By any measure, governments that have implemented communism or socialism—by attempting to control and manipulate economies to achieve equality—have been dismal failures. They rarely last more than a few decades and have never ended peacefully. Managing the thousands and thousands of inputs and outputs that make a free-market economy work efficiently is not possible. Even if it were, the intricacies of such precisely managed financial systems require much more control than monarchies of old, leading to deeply ensconced power structures that enable fascism, where the state itself becomes a god to be worshiped, justified in any action—no matter how brutal—to achieve the common good. To add to the citizen's misery, where advances in technology provided hope for political and economic progress, it also supplied governments with the improved ability to kill their own citizens en masse—a hallmark event of communist and socialist regimes as their dreams of an egalitarian state begin to collapse.

The zeal for which many intelligent humans desire fairness is clearly visible throughout their willingness to reconsider economic models of redistribution again and again, despite all evidence that such policies are ineffective at creating anything besides starvation and elevated body counts. Nevertheless, human pride and the dream of equality persists and blinds each new generation with the promise that "this time, it will be different."

A problem with communism and socialism is that they don't even pretend to benefit or improve the creation of wealth, something capitalism has excelled at like nothing else. Because men are more skilled at acquiring things and women at their redistribution, the modern world's transition into a predominantly matriarchal society favors the increasing likelihood of failed socialist states—America, chief amongst them.

The most grievous error those who champion these collectivist ideals make is the mistaken concept that the economy is a fixed pool of money that can never grow. Free-market systems are able to more efficiently convert scarce resources like materials and labor (your time) into something useful. By so doing, these efficiencies translate into more wealth; more jobs, more profit, and to the disdain of many—more inequality. Under capitalism, more people gain more wealth. It is not an even distribution of these resources, to be sure, but for those who work hard and smart, the likelihood they will be able to provide for their families is high.

Part of the reason many on the left hate America is likely because it so clearly highlights the failures of communism and socialism. The belief that someone can make a good living based on the quality or quantity of their work—and not some inherited social status—is surprisingly new. For thousands of years humanity lived mired within abject poverty, due in part to powerful monarchies or dictators who directed the output of nearly everyone's work as they saw fit. The economic miracle that America helped provide inverted this long-standing trap and gave nearly anyone the ability to rise far above the station into which they were born. It no longer mattered what family you came from. It no longer mattered what race you were. If you were willing to put in the work, you would likely be rewarded.

Unfortunately, the incredible prosperity this shift provided has been forgotten—despised by an ungrateful populace obsessed with equality above all else. The result is that while our founding economic model of capitalism may be taught in schools and universities, it is under the guise of hatred and loathing. It may have created remarkable wealth, so much that our poorest citizens live greater than kings and queens did just two hundred years ago—but that doesn't matter. Some got more than others, and because of that, the system must be destroyed. In the effort of fairness, they will remove the most-desired top floor with the penthouse view, unaware they will have just created a new penthouse view, one floor lower. Eventually, after enough fairness has been dealt, the building—and the country— will be gone, replaced with socialism's most notorious effects: Rations. Food lines. Death and despair.

We have already lost much of the original soul of our country and the cracks are beginning to show. The American ideals of personal liberty, limited government, and capitalism are *not* naturally occurring—they must be carefully and purposefully instilled in every new generation of people born into this place. "The student has not learned what the teacher has not taught," the saying goes, and we, as citizens, parents, and educators have neglected our students, our children, our neighbors. We have not taught them the miracle of America's creation. We have not made them thankful for the incredible gifts they've been given. As a result, the peace and prosperity we enjoyed for over two hundred years is being stripped away —all in the name of equality.

While the disruption of traditional gender roles and economic stability should move anyone concerned for their children's future to action, something else is happening which should concern you even more—a foul deception that has the potential to cause more suffering than anything, a lie by which even the Church itself has become consumed.

The Call

In Naples, Florida, members of the First Baptist Church experienced something very strange. In early 2019, their long-time Senior Pastor announced his retirement, a statement that set off a sequence of events that revealed major disagreements which had formed within their church body. As they were a large congregation—with a huge operating budget and staff to manage—the search committee set some lofty expectations. Amongst other qualifications, their guidelines stipulated they were looking for someone who had senior pastor experience leading a church with at least 1,200 members for over five years. Out of one hundred candidates, they whittled the submissions down to two men—both of whom evidently sensed trouble brewing at the church and withdrew their applications.

The committee ended up "issuing a call" to Marcus Hayes, a junior pastor from one of the original two applicant's church. He was not a senior pastor, but considered a teaching pastor who led a smaller satellite location of a larger church body. As the congregation began to hear word of the search committee's decision, they became concerned he did not meet the qualifications originally specified—concerns which appeared to be largely ignored. Additional research began to turn up social media activity that troubled some of First Baptist's members. Hayes was posting articles and messages in support of politicians and religious leaders that openly supported abortion and race-based social justice initiatives, ideologies that were at odds with their beliefs.

When Hayes arrived weeks later in Naples to preach over the weekend, the air was thick with tension. The search committee had continued to push forward, confident Hayes was the man God had chosen to lead their congregation despite the misgivings of many. After each of several services Hayes preached at, members filled out a ballot as to whether they wanted him as their next pastor. Church by-laws stipulated he had to receive 85% of the vote to get the position, but to the committee's horror, he did not. Nineteen percent of the congregation had voted against him, meaning he could not legally be hired.

This story might have ended there but exploded into chaos because of the church leadership's ensuing reaction. The story might have ended there, but became national news because Marcus Hayes is black and the congregation he was to serve was predominantly white. Despite manifest concerns with his qualifications and politically liberal leanings, the Naples church leadership exploded with anger, insisting the dissenting members who voted against him did so because they were racist.

The leadership was so embarrassed over the vote, they wrote a public letter to their denomination, the Southern Baptist Convention, apologizing for the racist members amongst them. "If all things had been equal and fair," the letter went, "our story would not have reached far and wide," a curious thing to say given the dramatic denomination-wide message it was mentioned within. Not content to stop there, members who voted against Hayes were identified and began receiving letters that their church membership had been terminated— excommunicated, in a sense, without any due process or chance to defend themselves. At last check, the First Baptist Naples leadership had hired powerful attorneys to defend their decisions and were expected to attempt to hire Marcus Hayes anyway.

Our world—nearly our entire planet—is obsessed with racism. Definitions seem to change by the day, but nearly everyone is convinced that ending human's propensity for prejudice or discrimination based on skin color to be the most important quest of the modern era. It is a peculiar fascination because scientists—and those who study race—have recently declared the results of extensive human genome research: We are all one race, they determined. We are only .2% different, genetically speaking, and most of those differences have nothing to do with physical appearance. For a culture that applauds diversity like nothing else, it's unclear why this minuscule variance in human DNA—a clear indication of sameness—would be cause for celebration. It takes a special mind to rejoice in our differences while at the same time celebrating the scientific discovery that perhaps after all we are not so different.

This ideological schizophrenia is apparent in those who speak about—and seek to put an end to—racism. "Celebrate diversity," the mantra goes, hastily Sharpie'd on thousands of poster-boards across college campuses everywhere. "We are all one race," they read on the back—their blue-haired authors seemingly eager to sustain this impossible dichotomy at fever pitch for the rest of their lives. In an effort to avoid their possible wrath, corporations populate their advertising with a manufactured diversity that any other country would find comical. Marketing materials for universities are the worst offenders—their unicorn-hopes clearly visible by the rainbow skin tones present in every commercial or brochure they produce. Books are written, videos are edited, and documentaries have been made—all dedicated to highlighting, explaining, and exposing the greatest sin: racism.

Racism is also apparently unique by the fact you need not have ever perpetrated, conducted, or even thought a racist thing in your life. By mere luck, you may have been born into a culture where racism runs amok—even though you might not see it—and for that, there is serious work to be done. This is a curious component of racism that you may have not realized. In an irony difficult to comprehend, despite the minute genetic differences which span all of humanity, only a tiny sliver of that human spectrum is actually capable of racism. In fact, this slice of people are incapable of *not being racist*. It is literally in their DNA—a genetic fate which has doomed them to a life of relentless racism. If the happenstance of their birth had produced slightly more or less melanin, their skin tones would be slightly different and they would not suffer this defect. The world would be able to conduct its affairs in peace and harmony, far from the evil grip of such prejudice.

Unfortunately, some people are born Caucasian. European. White. A magical mixture of melanin which triggers the appearance of a mysterious racism gene. As a result, that particular race, people group or ethnicity comes prepackaged with the mother of all sins—a grievance so horrible neither God nor Jesus could even address it in the Bible.

If you haven't been paying much attention to modern conversations about racism, you may not pick up on the sarcasm of what I'm saying. If you *have* been paying attention, you're probably aware that racism has been declared a one-way street. Apparently, most ethnicities are incapable of being racist—only Caucasians have the ability. Hispanics cannot be racist. Africans cannot be racist. "People of color," as the saying goes, "cannot be racist." White people, they'll tell you, control the levers of power— the machinery by which racism infiltrates everything. Without this power, this imbalance, racism would be impossible. This is why you may be racist without even meaning to be. If you were plopped on the proverbial deserted island, without a non-Caucasian for hundreds of miles, only then might you be incapable of being racist.

What is going on with this obvious madness? Why has our country—over 150 years after slavery was abolished— taken such an intense turn for the worse? Like the other topics covered in this book, I believe the answer can be traced directly to our obsession with equality.

Dilemma

In 1971, Coca-Cola aired a new commercial, the most expensive that had ever been produced. From atop a hill in Mansion, Italy, a multi-cultural cast, all holding bottles of Coke labeled in their native languages, sang together:

I'd like to buy the world a home, and furnish it with love.
Grow apple trees and honey bees, and snow white turtle doves.
I'd like to teach the world to sing in perfect harmony.
I'd like to buy the world a Coke, and keep it company.

The sentimental lyrics of love and harmony reflected the hippy culture of the day, but as the closing aerial shot revealed hundreds of Europeans, Africans, Asians and Latin Americans singing together, a new chapter in the quest for world peace was born. The ad incredibly powerful, the equivalent of a modern-day viral phenomenon, the song so popular it was re-recorded (minus the Coca-Cola reference) and on the radio within two weeks, peaking at #13 on Billboard charts.

Twenty years later, when the ad was reshot for the Super Bowl with the same actors and their grown children, the promise of diversity and a multi-cultural utopia had reached new heights. But it was not to be. Within a year, Los Angeles was consumed in fire as racially-motivated riots and arson devastated the city. Four white police officers had been acquitted for the brutal beating of an unarmed black motorist named Rodney King and someone had videotaped the whole incident. Anyone who could stand watching the clip would never forget the sickening billy-club blows reigning down on King's body. Somehow, the jury pronounced the officers not guilty.

After the verdicts were announced, the ensuing anger from residents of Los Angeles bubbled over into full-blown riots, looting, arson, and violence. Over 1,100 buildings were destroyed, the damage totaling almost $1 billion. Sixty-three people would be killed, leading King to hold an emotional press conference, imploring the city for calm by asking, "Can we all just get along? Can we get along? We're all stuck here for a while. Let's try to work it out."

There is a glaring, obvious truth modern society has found itself unable to acknowledge: racial inequality is a naturally occurring phenomenon. There are genetic differences between us, starting at the most obvious—physical characteristics—that extend well beyond and span the range of human experience. If you've attended an orchestra concert recently, you may have noticed a majority of string players were of Asian descent. If you've watched a football game, you will know that besides the placekicker, both teams are likely to feature predominantly black athletes.

There are many racial stereotypes that are impossible to ignore—patterns of appearance and behavior that define and differentiate us as humans. Of course there are outliers, but to insist that all races are equal is ridiculous. Equal in God's sight? Yes, of course—few would question that presumption. But equal in all things, universally interchangeable within any situation? To believe and insist on this, as many people do, is to ignore reality.

Ethnicities have many other differences besides the hue of their skin. Throughout the United States are hundreds of ethnic enclaves—Chinatowns, Little Havanas and Little Saigons—all of them tight-knit groups of people who have chosen to live in close proximity not only because their skin colors matched or their eyes were shaped the same, but because of many similarities, most of which extend beyond obvious physical characteristics. In much of the world, this kind of discussion would not be thought of as controversial in any way, but instead would be considered an obvious—even innocuous—truth. However, amongst "progressive" populations committed to the belief that all people are born with the same gifts and deficiencies, these same statements might cajole some into uncontrollable rage.

There is probably nothing more vexing to modern humans than the dilemma of racial inequality. They want so badly for things to be fair. To be even. Christians, who have been promised unity in Christ, struggle with this more than anyone. We struggle to understand why God would have created a world in which certain people groups accel at certain things and are deficient in others. "Jesus loves the little children," we sing, "all the children of the world. Red, brown, yellow, black and white, they are precious in his sight," yet inequality stares us in the face, an incongruity we are unable to reconcile.

As the current thinking goes, if all races are equal, yet one group consistently bubbles to the top in a few categories, there obviously *must* have been something nefarious they did for it to happen. *White privilege* is often pointed to as the cause, an undefinable boogeyman always surfacing wherever it can create the most harm—as clear an example of racism if there ever was one. For those who are unable to accept racial inequality as a naturally-occurring phenomenon, they must be able to conjure all manner of spirits to explain its presence, and white privilege has become the cause *du jour*.

And so white privilege is called forth by the shamans within and without Christendom. Amongst traditional churches and denominations across our country, this new way of thinking about racism—critical race theory—has been gaining steam. Denominations are making dedicated efforts to rid their congregations of racism, going to great lengths to prove to the world they are "pure." Even conservative churches—who bravely confront delicate issues such as promoting traditional male leadership or resisting LGBTQ-affirming policies—have been unable to resist the onslaught for fear of being labeled racist.

Those who fan the flames of racism insist it to be a special type of sin, something much different than your run-of-the-mill problem with pride, greed, or envy—an affront so heinous not even the blood of Jesus Christ on the Cross can fully atone. Churches, denominations, and even seminaries are hosting "white privilege" workshops, conferences, and curriculums to try and exorcise the demons of racism that witch doctors have diagnosed them with. They bend the knee to coddle professional agitators who come amongst them insisting that racism requires something else—many other things, in fact, to correct, amend, or redress: guilt-ridden confessionals or financial reparations—pathetic indulgences for which even medieval Catholic popes would be ashamed to take payment.

With racism, those who reject inequality as an intentional component of creation have found a weakness they can incessantly exploit—a missing scale in the underbelly of a great dragon that provides a pathway through which their rebellion may find a home. Like Rodney King, many Christians want to "just get along" so badly they are falling on their own sword in hopes the shaman are right. But their efforts—all of them—will be in vain. The bride of Christ will ultimately persevere but these once-great churches—now steered by weak men and women who seek to please the world rather than God— they will fall.

Like and Love

Sitting at the bottom of a huge tree of human diversity is race and ethnicity. It is the single biggest differentiator between any group of humans besides gender. As you make your way up through the trunk, you would pass through culture, language, and morals. Towards the top, you might find a dear friend, a unicorn, who shared both your love of, say, pumpkin-spice lattes *and* Tolkien. If you were to trace that friend back down the tree, you probably wouldn't be surprised to find you originated from the same branch far below. You presumably come from the same culture, you likely speak the same language, and unsurprisingly, you are probably a similar ethnicity. This isn't a guarantee, of course, but the likelihood that two tiny twigs next to each other at the top of a tree come from different branches far below is minute.

The outcome of this branching structure is a tendency to be more comfortable around humans who are similar to us. It is an odd feature of modern dialogue that this statement even needs to delicately explained, but the unfortunate truth is that life is hard and humans have a propensity to blame others more unlike themselves for their suffering. As philosopher and economist Friedrich Hayek put it, humans are still programmed to understand the world in personal and tribal terms.

Because of this, there will always be social friction. Customers jump counters and attack fast-food cashiers for getting their orders wrong. Parents come to blows over hurt feelings from Little League baseball games. Even intimate family Thanksgivings are ruined by brothers and sisters and mothers and fathers screaming at each other over perceived slights. Every day across the country, humans respond with outbursts and violence when their anger at what may seem to be the slightest offense boils over.

The more profound the difference, the easier it is to find fault with someone. The more profound their differences, the further both parties have to reach to maintain unity on a given issue. If blood relatives—who are the same race, believe in the same God, live in the same house, and both root for the same sports teams—are capable of fighting over the most trivial difference of opinion, it is not hard to imagine why those with much less in common might not get along.

I've listened to probably a hundred sermons on racism and have heard several well-intentioned pastors pose different versions of the same question, asking "When's the last time you ate lunch with someone who didn't look like you? When's the last time you had someone—*inside* your house—who looked different than you?" An extended pause of silence inevitably follows, the pastor's accusatory gaze intended to drive home the dagger of racism.

The reality of the human condition is bleak, for we are much worse than racist. We are guilty of sin infinitely worse than racism. For instance, to spend time with someone who wants to talk basketball when you'd prefer to talk theology can be annoyance enough to decline a lunch invitation. You couldn't bear the thought of spending an hour with this sports junkie who couldn't tell the difference between a Calvinist or an Arminian if it killed him, yet you'd never be taken to task for this slight in church—a dear friend who wants to spend time with you but is unable simply because you can't relate to their sports predilection.

Even more concerning—marriages are failing everyday, families ripped apart, damage which ripples across generations but inside the church, such divisions would never warrant a dressing down from the pulpit. Pastors are often more concerned about the egregious sin of not liking everyone.

Let me say something many seemed to have forgotten: We don't have to like each other. We are called to love each other, and yes, love each other—we must try to do that. We can build houses. We can feed the hungry. We can clothe the homeless. We can comfort those who lost a loved one. We can share a difficult truth with someone who needs correction. We can drive swamp boats through flooded streets to rescue elderly couples stuck in their attic, desperately clinging to life. We can move to a foreign country, putting our careers on hold and our family's lives at risk, in hopes of delivering a steady supply of water and Jesus to those who need it most. We can do all these things —sacrifices of service God has called us to do—we can do those all day every day for the next 20 years but guess what? We don't have to like each other. And in fact, we're probably not going to.

Coworkers won't always like each other. Church members won't always like each other. Elders or deacons won't always like each other. Even family members—our own flesh and blood—we won't always like each other. As Christians, we are called to love our neighbor as ourselves, and we should make every attempt, no matter how many times we fall short. But to suggest that it is profoundly sinful that someone would prefer to spend their time with another person who is more like them than not? This is a non-existent offense, a phantom sin conjured from thin air purely for its ability to induce guilt and shame in the accused and signal virtue and righteousness in the accuser. Satan, the great accuser, must be proud.

If the concept of not liking everyone strikes you as offensive, know that outside of progressive matriarchal societies most people would accept it as completely normal. Throughout much of the world where ethnic groups may live in close proximity, they are still typically separated by their religious institutions, schools, businesses, and many other things. There is occasional overlap, of course, but in general, the notion that Arabs in Israel may want a different education for their children than Orthodox Jews is uncontroversial. Government officials wouldn't attempt to come up with a public school curriculum that satisfied both parties, knowing it to be an exercise in futility that would only lead to more conflict. Instead, they allow flexibility between them, each group determining for themselves the subjects their children will study. The one-size-fits-all approach of the United States and other liberal countries—where all people groups are assumed (or forced) to be identical—will not create peace or increased understanding, no matter how hard we may try. In fact, it will do the opposite. It will create enmity and division for everyone involved.

The lens through which modern racism is viewed—white privilege—may prove to be one of the most destructive ideologies of our time. It is one thing to accept and teach that various people groups are different from each other, but what is being whispered in churches and shouted outside them is something entirely different. Generations of people will have been taught their lives are infinitely less than what they were meant to be, the only reason because of the actions of a particular race—a diabolic accusation whose violent effects are only just beginning to show. To propose that a nationality or religious group might be the cause of someone's suffering would provide enough kindling for a terrible fire. To insist a particular *race* of people did it—that is enough gasoline for war.

White privilege—as an accusation—is simply the admission that there is racial inequality but the rejection that a particular situation may be God's intent. I'll say it again another way, because this is really important: Churches who preach about—and apologize for—white privilege are able to admit there are racial differences, but refuse to accept God could have designed things this way on purpose.

Is there Asian privilege in Asia? Is there African privilege in Africa? Surely the native residents of various continents sport advantages over immigrants, but for some reason, you rarely hear such things spoken of. There is no mention of African privilege. There is no reference to Asian or Hispanic or Jewish privilege—only white privilege. Why is this? God loves his children equally and shows no favor. I believe that, like the song says, we are *all* precious in his sight. To suggest that a single race is cursed—in a perpetual state of sin which no other ethnicity is capable of engaging in—is clearly counter to how the Bible describes creation.

The indoctrination of churches with white privilege and its atonement ritual—racial reconciliation—are devious attempts to destroy Christendom from within. They have planted deep the seeds of hate and guilt where there should have been none. They have created a new type of transgression, a man-made sin that affects only one race of people and appears to place them outside the forgiveness God provided all others.

The accusations of modern racism, rooted in rebellion against God's natural order, have twisted human's desire for peace and unity into a indictment of an entire race of people. Beyond that, they have taken over the church and created an auxiliary gospel—the social gospel—whose works-based merit system will inevitably turn many believers away from the saving work of Jesus on the Cross, a rejection God is not likely to stand for.

The Racism Delusion

When I was in college, a few Christian organizations got together to hold a nightly week-long revival. I had been asked to play the piano and in preparation for being able to accompany the gospel-style service, went along with a friend to listen in on her Sunday church meeting. I was the only white person there, a strange sensation, even for me— someone who attended heavily minority schools my entire life.

"There's the piano over there," she said as we entered the rapidly-filling sanctuary, passing by a table full of hand-held fans with the pastor's picture on them.

"That's a pretty piano," I thought to myself.

"You can go ahead and start playing until they're ready to go," she said, unaware I thought I was there only to listen, and had planned on hiding in the back so as not to cause a disturbance.

"I'm sorry, what?" I asked, my heart pounding. "Play what?"

"Just jump in there and get us going," she said, giving me an encouraging slap on the shoulder.

People who have recurring dreams often point to a traumatic event they feel may have created a repeating pattern of fear expressed while they sleep. For me, being the only white person there was not it. It was walking down the aisle to the front of a black church in my junky clothes and sitting down at the piano, rocking back and forth in silence as I tried to think of something—anything—I could play that might not offend their gospel sensibilities, the drummer's dramatic cymbal rolls doing nothing to lessen my crippling anxiety. As a result, my dreams frequently involve me being late for an event in which I'm supposed to play—a performance for which I've done no preparation and typically can't even locate my instrument.

Regardless, in the time since then—and because of that event—I've become more adept at playing gospel music. My wife and I even considered joining an all-black church we frequently attended soon after getting married. You may believe this to be a virtue-signaling story intent upon deflecting any claims of racism laid upon me, but it is not. I freely admit I was uncomfortable. I did not grow up with gospel music and did not know the songs. I did not grow up with 3-hour long services and would get restless halfway through. Despite the warmth I was received with, I could not help feeling that I was an outsider, attempting to force myself into a culture and church body I had no familiarity with. It never occurred to me they may have felt the same.

We have been trying to end racism and discrimination for over 150 years. We've launched thousands of programs, taught hundreds of thousands of classes, and spent millions —if not billions—of dollars in an attempt to root out this thorn in humanity's side. Why has nothing worked? Why does it feel like we're starting from square one sometimes, despite everyone's herculean efforts to end this scourge?

The progressive left's definition of racism as someone who may occasionally benefit from *inequality* has allowed them to target anyone as bigoted with impunity. Even a more sober description of racism—a preference for people similar to yourself, from your own tribe, if you like—has inexplicably been rejected by many within our nation and faith as an egregious sin. I want to ask you to consider a difficult question: Using this more accurate definition of the word—a preference for people who are more similar to yourself than not—what if humans were designed to be "racist?" What if racism is God's desire?

"But racism is part of the Fall," many Christians will say. "Before Adam and Eve ate from the Tree of Knowledge, racism wouldn't have existed." It might not have existed, but it's impossible to know because there was only one race at that time. It's difficult to be racist when everyone is the same race as yourself.

What about later, when there *were* multiple ethnicities, you might ask? According to Genesis, God purposefully divided humanity into different tribes after the flood. They had all been speaking one language and were attempting to build a tower that reached heaven, the tower of Babel, as it is called. God was displeased with their pride and scattered them over the entire earth, giving them different languages to speak to ensure their separation. Was this punishment? Or something different—foresight, perhaps?

As a result, these tribes learned to stay apart from each other. Why? Because when their paths did cross, there was often brutal fighting. Nations were defined by ethnicity and culture, long before borders or a geographical area factored into the equation. And the Bible is full of nations— different tribes—fighting against each other, with death and destruction the result.

So when David pleads "Keep me safe, God," in Psalm 16, he rejoices by saying, "The boundary lines have fallen in pleasant places for me; truly, I have a beautiful heritage." He took comfort in the safety that his nation could easily be protected from invaders. He was not concerned about getting along with other tribes. You'll find no Psalms where David calls out to God for forgiveness for harboring mistrust towards other nations, for thinking of them differently than his own. They were often a threat to him, and he called upon the LORD for protection.

It is completely natural to have a preference for those of your own "tribe" or ethnicity over others. This isn't just partiality for people who have a similar skin-tone, despite what many insist, but a profound kinship driven by many different things. One can see why those on the left abhor the concept of borders or nationhood altogether—under this definition, racism is the prerequisite to nationalism. It is not an optional, "wouldn't it be great if we had it" kind of thing, but an essential requirement for building and sustaining a nation—an institution created by God, apparently to minimize conflict and provide safety and security for its citizens.

This concept will be very difficult for the modern Christian to consider. They may insist that nations exist by virtue of a disconnected group of people who share a common ideal—no matter their ethnicity, language, or any other distinction. This concept, called *civic nationalism*, is a recent invention whose limits are currently being discovered throughout America as cities are burnt to the ground in the name of "justice." A common belief alone—

even if religious in nature—has never been enough to sustain a nation for long.

The modern Christian may also point to Galatians 3:28, where it says, "There is neither Jew nor Greek, there is neither slave nor free, there is no male and female, for you are all one in Christ Jesus." This verse was making it clear that Jesus the Messiah's offer of salvation was not for the Jewish people alone, but everyone—a bit of doctrine many were having trouble understanding at that time. It was not an admonition against nationalism, and certainly had nothing to do with a proclivity for wanting to live amongst similar people. After the tower of Babel, these institutions were never questioned—they were accepted as a logical division, necessary to maintain peace between frequently warring tribes.

Some will point to Leviticus 19:33-34: "When a stranger sojourns with you in your land, you shall not do him wrong. You shall treat the stranger who sojourns with you as the native among you, and you shall love him as yourself, for you were strangers in the land of Egypt." Sojourn refers to a temporary visit, meaning not permanent. Regardless, this verse is not an admonition against nations or a preference of your own tribe over others. It was a call to be kind to others traveling through your land—treating them as you would your own kind.

Certainly a beautiful bit of scripture that I don't imagine many have a problem with, provided of course, the visitors are not meaning to harm you. And provided their visit is temporary. "Thank you for leaving," as my father likes to say towards the end of get-togethers—to members of his own family.

One final bit of scripture, from Acts 17 as Paul and Silas and Timothy are working hard to establish the early Christian church. From verses 26 and 27: "And he made from one man every nation of mankind to live on all the face of the earth, having determined allotted periods and the boundaries of their dwelling place, that they should seek God, in the hope that they might feel their way toward him and find him. Yet he is actually not far from each one of us…" Again, the Bible promotes nations and boundaries as a positive institution, a foundation for enabling believers to seek God.

You will often hear people mention heaven, or the kingdom of God, as inspiration for their dedication to ending racism, and by extension nationalism or nationhood altogether. "We'll all get along in heaven," they'll say, confident they know the manner God will employ to achieve it. "So because we are Christians, we should be able to get along with anyone—right now." This is completely foolish and will end in death and misery for many thousands of people.

Objections will, no doubt, be raised from multi-cultural churches, who may point to their incredible worship services as evidence of what can be accomplished when people of various ethnicities get together and put God above all else. Like many others, I've been touched by these moving tributes of unity. There are exceptions to every rule, of course, and although worship through music can bridge many divides, outside the church, when the music stops, the solidarity often evaporates. We should carefully understand what God has done—what he ordained— before we go tempting fate because of our own pride.

Nowhere in the Bible do we find declarations that nationhood is wrong. Nowhere in the Bible do we find any insinuation that a preference to live amongst your own— what many call racism—is wrong. We do find frequent mention that God created divisions and boundaries, scattering people amongst different geographical regions and languages. We do find frequent mention of God's people calling on him for protection from invaders who meant to harm them. They would have never welcomed foreigners into their midst because they believed a future promise of peace in the kingdom of God would protect them from harm. Who are we to insist that nationhood as described throughout the Bible will cease to exist in the kingdom of God? Who are we to insist that David's pleasant boundary lines were an anomaly that will serve no purpose in the kingdom? For all we know, the kingdom may feature nations, races, and languages *more* prominently rather than less.

Today might be considered a repeat of Genesis 11. We have built the tower of Babel anew, not with brick and tar, but with multiculturalism and equality. We have assured each other that there is no height we cannot achieve, no division amongst us we cannot overcome, if only we work hard enough to overcome it. God will not be mocked and because of that, the unwinding of this supreme arrogance is unfortunately likely to be very painful.

Already, the division and mayhem brought about from mixing peoples with reckless abandon is causing death and destruction. A single race—the very race which championed such multiculturalism in the first place—has been assigned as the scapegoat, with outbursts of violence against them, the frequent result. "Whiteness is wicked," theologian Ekemini Uwan said to hundreds of women at a recent worship conference with nary an ounce of reservation or unease. Did those listening to her agree? Christian pulpits across the country often deliver sermons that would make it seem so.

This sort of thing will continue. It will get worse. Scriptures have given us clear warnings against this kind of experiment—in the first book of the Bible, no less. And we have ignored them. We have insisted that despite the warnings of the Bible, despite the divisions and borders that God purposefully created, we can and will get along, no matter the cost.

The first time "racism" was mentioned in our Supreme Court was in 1944. It wouldn't be mentioned again until 1967. Just three years earlier, president Lyndon B. Johnson had declared war on poverty. Since that time, we've spent $22 trillion dollars to end poverty and the have-nots are madder than ever. Who knows how much we've spent on ending racism?

We still have poverty. We still have racism. Perhaps all our money has been a waste. Race and ethnicities were created by God. Division and borders, languages and separation—all created by God. Perhaps it's not too late we stopped defying him. The tower will come down—one way or another. I pray it's peaceful. I pray that God will be merciful to those who honor him when this experiment comes crashing to the ground.

This is a lengthy and sobering take on the issue of racism and white privilege, but believe it or not, this represents but the tip of the spear, the beginning of a long descent into hell as God's people reject his natural order for a design of their own making. Just like our rejection of naturally-occurring gender and economic inequality, our insistence on recasting creation within the framework of our own understanding—rather than God's—may cost us dearly.

Church

I have described three areas where our quest for equality is destroying modern civilization: gender, the economy, and race—but there are many others. For instance, our deeply-rooted love of animals has transformed into near-perversion. When my wife and I lived in Los Angeles, we joked that locals would have children only to make sure they were ready for the responsibilities of dog ownership. More recently, fanatics have taken to storming restaurants, dumping blood on its patrons to protest a natural desire to eat meat. Politicians have sympathized with them, vowing to tax or ban certain animal products.

Parents have completely lost the plot on raising their sons and daughters, treating them as equal members of every decision-making process, unable to accept that perhaps their children were born unwise and in need of careful instruction. With many kids missing a father completely, their mother incapable of discipline, the likelihood many of them will help destroy our country—rather than sustain it—is certain.

An even stranger phenomenon can be seen in the sphere of mental health as bestiality, pedophilia, and homosexuality—once considered deviant behavior and possible evidence of neurological dysfunction—are being normalized as the common practice of a healthy society. Even those who suffer from autism, possibly one of the greatest medical tragedies of the modern age, are being reframed as completely normal, simply in need of better understanding rather than medical or scientific aid—all under the dark cloud of equality.

The twisted dichotomy appears everywhere you look. "We are all unique," a parent might insist, as their 10-year-old cross-dressing son dances for the grown men tucking dollar bills into his waistband. Others might proclaim with indignation, "If a few are sick, then no one will be sick," as all manner of mental illness is redefined into oblivion.

Just as we have lost our ability to confront mental illness, our country is being flooded with immigrants from cultures and traditions that are completely at odds with the Christian underpinnings of America. Despite their unwillingness to assimilate in any way—a universal requirement for maintaining the fabric of any country—they are welcomed with open arms. Because of this, America is full of disparate people groups who can't even understand each other. This most basic of all commonalities—language—is missing and yet we expect them to understand and accept the nuances of our culture and tradition.

"All cultures are equal," a judge might announce, "but the defendant didn't understand that raping children was wrong," as she releases an immigrant from jail after serving a paltry 3-week sentence. Not content to be outdone, Christians have joined in, hosting sanctuaries for their future conquerors—eager to ensure everyone of their commitment to equality. Well-intentioned denominations have accepted the call and have joined hand-in-hand with strange bedfellows such as the National Immigration Forum (funded by George Soros) in its pursuit.

This is to say nothing of the social justice initiatives growing like cancer throughout our congregations. The never-ending quest for equality supposes that not only can the price of millions of products be centrally controlled in a fair manner, but the balance of vice and virtue, work and reward—every human emotion—can adequately be redistributed in such a way that equality is achieved, a vain pursuit which will end in sorrow.

For how do we make equal intellect, beauty, or physical ability? Compassion? Empathy? How about other virtues? Pride? Forgiveness? Joy? We cannot. Social justice initiatives inevitably must focus on wealth and in so doing ignore much of what makes someone happy. It reduces humans to consumers of money and supposes that equality in this one regard is sufficient to make everyone happy. The reality is—it doesn't. It allows those who blindly advocate for equality assuage their guilt, if only temporarily, but does nothing to adjust the natural inequality that permeates every cell of every living organism on the planet.

In the 1800s, the sermons of pastors across the United States were often consumed with their greatest fear—atheism. A time was coming, they'd warn, when men would no longer declare that God even exists. They didn't realize there was a far greater threat—infiltration, rather than invasion—that would transform Christians amongst every denomination across this once great country. Men would not question if God exists, but rather whether he really meant the things he said in the Bible. "Perhaps we got it wrong?" they now ask. "Perhaps he didn't mean to condemn sin after all?"

The echoes of the serpent should be obvious. They are as loud today as they ever were. "We are all sinners," Christians today might say, "but some can't help it"—the inevitable outcome of a people who cannot square the reality of inequality. The social justice gospel, despite an insistence on equality, insinuates that certain individuals are *not* responsible for their own behavior—meaning their sin is not their responsibility but someone else's, a new category of sin not described in the Bible, one that can come into existence (and evaporate) based on someone else's feeling or experience.

Some churches have turned their focus so profoundly on racism and other perceived "oppression" they have lost sight of the Gospel message altogether. Repentance or redemption are rarely mentioned. Sin is used only to frame the inescapable racism of being white, while prayers are offered to God for "justice," not salvation. These churches are Christian in name only and can only stomach mentioning Jesus so long as liberation of the oppressed comes across as his major life's work.

This has created an army of believers who cannot truly love anyone. They may feed them, clothe them, and coddle them in every imaginable way but when push comes to shove, many Christians will not be able to break the cold, hard truth to them: They are sinners, just like everyone else and without the saving work of Jesus on the Cross, will fall short of God's grace—the one equality we all share.

End

The common mousetrap is made up of several different parts. Every component is completely different. Some are large, some are small. Some are wooden, some are metal. Some can bend, while others cannot. They all have a particular position in which they are supposed to fit together. But without each and every piece working exactly as it was designed, you don't catch fewer mice—you catch *none*. No matter which part is missing, if even one of them is lost, the trap ceases to function *at all*.

Complementarians understand that a machine of identical parts would serve no purpose—no matter how many pieces there were. Imagine trying to make a mousetrap out of 15 identical pieces of wood or metal. This would never work, no matter their shape. Instead, it would require a variety of pieces—each working together for a common cause according to their various distinctions.

The careful design of God's creation frustrates many. You cannot have both diversity *and* equality—you must pick one. The more diverse your population, the more unequal it will be and the more social discord and mistrust will likely result. The more equality you are able to foster, the less diversity you are likely to have. Modern man wants both, and appears content to drive himself insane with the mistaken belief he can somehow achieve it. At universities and corporations throughout the world, entire educational departments, government offices, and corporate endowments are dedicated to achieving the impossible: Diversity *and* equality. It is no wonder these people often speak like escaped inmates from an asylum.

Many pagans worship at the altar of diversity but mistakenly believe that, through human endeavor, equality can also be achieved. It cannot, and as I hope I've made clear by now, it has lead to ruin through our attempts. It was folly to meddle with creation in ways we didn't understand. Vaccines have inadvertently created thousands of man-made diseases in our attempt to control several naturally occurring ones. We have unwittingly created devastating environmental disasters in our attempt to extract power from where perhaps we should not have. All of these things are creating havoc but it is my suspicion none of these mistakes will end up causing as much devastation as our wholesale rejection of one of the most primal components of the entire cosmos—inequality. Wherever and whenever we step out too far, God's creation has pushed back harder than we expected, letting us know the limits of human comprehension. And so we have begun to see it now as we have reached the limits of man-made equality.

Thankfully, there is a better way—a much better way. If you accept that God's intent for creation is inequality—if you embrace that characteristic as the cornerstone trait of his grand design—a wonderful chrysalis will begin to form in your mind. A transformation will overtake you as you openly and willingly accept diversity—beautiful, specific, intentional variety within God's design. Throughout every nook and cranny of creation, the elaborate interplay of a million different components—from oxygen and carbon dioxide to men and women—will begin to testify to the truth that every single thing has been designed with a specific role that cannot be replicated by any other. We can try, of course, to redesign the machine—we can put spare parts where they ought not go—but as we can now clearly see, it will not work. We have broken much of creation and will be fortunate to get it working again.

As you journey along the arc of this realization, you should begin to see *yourself* differently—as a crucial component of God's grand design that slots in amongst the rest of creation in such a way that thousands of other pieces, parts, and people rely on *your* proper function to fulfill God's plan. It may not feel like that. It may feel like you are just a spare human that has been kept around for an emergency that never happened, for a song you learned but never got to sing, but I can assure you, this is not the case.

Early on Adam and Eve realized they occupied a rung on a ladder that placed them below God and in fact, were designed in such a way they *needed* God. But soon after, they would no doubt have realized that they needed each other. They were not meant to be alone, and just as we were designed to need God, we were made in such a way to need each other. Although we were created in his image, we are very different and without frequent upward-turned songs of praise to him, our hearts will find something else to elevate. In the same way, without a thorough appreciation of—and reliance on—our differences, our hearts will turn inward, away from God, and the prideful, selfishness of fallen creation will gain control.

From where you sit, you may not be able to see this. You may not be able to sense it or feel it, but you are as necessary to God's creation as the most significant person you can think of. And most importantly, your inequality— the ways in which God has made you different than others —is the reason why. Once you realize the world has been lying to you about how you and others should function within creation, a cloud of darkness will lift and you may find joy and happiness you cannot imagine.

Throughout our history, humans have struggled with the problem of sin: greed, lust, envy, gluttony. We clearly suffer from its effects everyday, but are uncomfortable in naming its source. It would seem *pride*, the one we tend to ignore—is, as the Bible suggests, the worst of them all. Like Adam and Eve first discovered, God has placed himself far above us, unequaled in his sovereignty. Unequaled in his holiness, his righteousness, or his justice. Unequaled in his love and mercy. Perhaps our ability to accept that we also are *not* like this—that most beautiful inequality of them all—perhaps that *will* one day be the source of all joy.

Epilogue

I hope it is obvious how many of America's cherished institutions are under attack. Decades ago, the church was active in helping to sustain the culture and traditions that contributed to its ranks. It was a symbiotic relationship. Those who attended worship services every Sunday morning taught their children the importance of the church, the Gospel, and the great country they were born into. But something broke along the way. Churches have forgotten what was given to them. They have become ungrateful.

With the birth of the United States, there was much to be thankful for. After having spent the majority of our existence in abject poverty and suffering, the human race was suddenly thrust on an upward arc of stability and prosperity. Within a short time, standards of living increased so dramatically that its poor would live better off than all but the richest of nobles had been just two hundred years earlier. Even slavery could not withstand the rising tide of American liberty and capitalism. The advent of a government whose purpose was to serve the people—rather than the other way around—coupled with a fervent commitment to the free exchange of goods and services of capitalism provided fertile soil to cultivate this miraculous transformation. It was a unique arrangement never before attempted. Economic and scientific progress vaulted our young country past many of its peers and our shores became the destination of choice for immigrants the world over.

Nestled within this journey was the constant presence of Christianity. Founding documents and patriotic hymns made frequent mention of what appeared to be divine intervention in the birth and rise of this great nation. Church services often expressed gratitude to God for the blessings the country was able to provide. They were right to give thanks—Americans enjoyed peace and prosperity other countries couldn't have dreamt of. Americans recognized their country was unique. They didn't attribute its success to random chance—a fortuitous collision of the right people on the right spot of land—but directly to God, the Father.

We often sing the first verse of our national anthem, but the final and fourth verse may provide clearer insight into the mood of the times:

Oh! thus be it ever, when freemen shall stand
Between their loved home and the war's desolation!
Blest with victory and peace, may the heav'n rescued land
Praise the Power that hath made and preserved us a nation.
Then conquer we must, when our cause it is just,
And this be our motto: "In God is our trust."
And the star-spangled banner in triumph shall wave
O'er the land of the free and the home of the brave!

Blessed with victory and peace, America was thought to have been rescued by heaven. But rescued from what, one might ask? Indians? Famine? The author was likely not speaking of violence or invaders but the scourge of civil unrest and abject poverty that had been the defining characteristic of humanity for most of its existence. America had broken the cycle of misery and oppression—something most believed to be impossible—and as a result, the Star-Spangled Banner's writer ascribes praise to "the Power" that both made and preserved this special nation. He then makes a special plea, a call for courage in the face of battle: Then conquer we must, when our cause it is just.

Who is it implying America must conquer? It was referring to the British—the old form of government whose soldiers were trying desperately to prevent the formation of this new country. The War of 1812 was upon them and the tiny nation of America was clinging desperately to the promise of what God had shown them. This wasn't really a war over land—there were seemingly limitless fields and forests. It wasn't a war over racial differences—the British and Americans were as genetically similar as any warring nations might be. It was war between the nations over the old way of doing things versus this new, experimental government that had upended centuries-old traditions of monarchies and dictatorship—the same type of rule nearly every other human since the dawn of creation had lived within.

America would win that war and persevere, and more songs would be written and sung throughout churches across the land:

America! America!
God shed his grace on thee,
And crown thy good with brotherhood
From sea to shining sea.

Americans knew what had been created was an incredible gift and treated it with the reverence it deserved. They didn't realize it at the time, but sustaining their country's existence would be most challenged not by wars with foreign powers, but its own citizens—future generations who would never experience the hopeless poverty from which America had arisen nor acknowledge the role their Christian faith had in founding the country. Without careful instruction, the miraculous transformation this new country provided faded into obscurity—in a sense, a victim of its own success. Later generations assumed the peace and prosperity capitalism had provided was the inevitable result of modern society rather than the carefully pruned system of beliefs that created it. They were wrong.

As it turned out, capitalism—and the nation of free men that enabled it—is not a naturally occurring phenomenon. In fact, the opposite is true. Dictators and monarchies have existed for thousands of years and until the last three hundred, no one really thought to question them. America presented an inverted model—where governmental rule existed to serve the people rather than the other way around. This incredible design worked perfectly for almost 250 years but is now fighting for its life as our fallen human nature guides us towards the oppressive systems of old.

The political strife and bickering destroying our way of life is due to a large group of people who insist that perhaps God got things wrong. That perhaps equality would have been a better model. They don't even realize it, but they long for a return to the dictatorship or monarchies of old. But rather than a crusty old man sitting high atop an iron throne, they are looking to place the state, or government, in his place. Even Christians are doing this—unaware of the ruin they are likely to bring upon our nation.

Humans are designed to look outward—to worship something—and without the God of Christendom to guide and give them meaning, many are pursuing their natural desire for significance and instruction from the government. Rather than thanking God our creator, they will sing anthems of praise to the state itself. Rather than looking inward to increase their compassion and charity, they look outward—to the government—to handle this for them. In all things, they have replaced normal religious conviction with a desire for the state to take its place—in worship, in instruction, in charity.

You might have sensed that things have been accelerating in the last few years—an increase in the number of people who openly call for socialist, communist or other forms of law and rule which are opposite from the things our country was founded on. You have probably noticed an increase in open hostility towards Christians in the past few years. Why is this happening so much now?

As more and more generations have left the faith, you will notice they are no longer rebelling against sin or Jesus but instead God's creation itself. The natural order of the world we live in is being challenged at every turn, and they seem to be winning. Nothing is safe from disruption and it should have become clear that inequality of anything or anyone will not be tolerated. They have been upending the natural order of God's creation for the last century and if we do not act, there may be nothing left to save.

In the last 20 years, this relentless quest has snowballed and begun to make our country nearly unrecognizable. The natural order of things is no longer being challenged but systematically destroyed piece by piece. It is no longer enough to question or upend traditional gender roles in our society. Now the notion of gender itself is being dismantled. They will tell you there are no males or females, just a long continuum of creatures that exist in between—and beyond.

Rather than celebrate what is beautiful, artists attempt to shock with the profane and grotesque. Musicians celebrate vice over virtue. Architects feel the tug and design buildings specifically in order they might *not* be considered beautiful. What was once considered mental illness has been rebranded as typical neurological development. Women are disfiguring their bodies, rejoicing in the destruction of their offspring. Men are embracing weakness and cowardice. The traditional family structure is ridiculed. And nearly all are celebrating wickedness. Celebrating violence. Celebrating the destruction of everything that is good.

Inevitably, this hunt to rid the world of inequality has landed at the doorstep of Christians—for we not only accept inequality but can embrace it as a crucial element in the natural order of God's design. We believe the various pieces and parts of God's creation are wonderfully designed to work with each other perfectly—a machine destined for failure when cogs try to work like axles and pulleys try to function as wheels. The distinct roles and duties of each and every man, woman, and child—even plants, animals, rivers and streams—were for most of human history thought to be self-evident. The constant affirmation of their grand design through cultural reminders and traditions seemed almost unnecessary. Unfortunately, they were.

We have completely squandered what was given to us. Without frequent celebration of the natural order—and due to incessant attacks by those who would destroy it, America and the Christian church itself feel nearly lost. These attacks have gained ground in the past few years because Christians are not actively defending the natural order—let alone the nation—God gave us. We have lived most of our lives in peace, our beliefs unchallenged. We have rarely needed to defend our faith and as a result, are content to spend our Sundays safely ensconced within the walls of our church buildings, deeply immersed in theological study or song. We dare not mention the enemy at the gates for fear it might scare the children. We pray for God to heal the sickness and disease of our members, never bothering to ask for a bit of help with the cancer that is destroying our entire church body from the inside.

The Christian church is collapsing under the incessant calls of equality. Denominations once considered stalwart defenders of the faith have folded like a house of cards as they openly pursue man-made remedies for man-made sin. Christians have begun to sing the song of equality, clearly visible in calls for social justice and racial reconciliation. While God has told us the path is narrow, we have widened it. "All are welcome" has become "None are guilty." And for a growing number of churches, it is not enough that man should accept Jesus as Savior—there are other sins, special transgressions, so egregious that Jesus on the Cross cannot save them from. They require artificial solutions in the form of diversity training or monetary reparations. These sins are also distinct in that one not even need to have committed them. Their forefathers need not have even committed them. These transgressions simply exist because of a faulty melanin count—in other words, because someone has the wrong skin color. Whether they know it, acknowledge it, or deny it, they have special privilege that confers a special sin for which even the Savior cannot atone—an accusation the great accuser is no doubt ecstatic to have planted deep within churches and denominations across our country.

If it is not already clear, the definitive target of the modern world's wrath is not just Christians, but white

Christian men—those seen as responsible for a terrible sin: the creation of the United States of America. An entire nation of opportunity where life, liberty, and the pursuit of happiness can provide a life others might only dream of having. Those without the talents—or desire—to pursue such lofty goals are left floating at the bottom of a rapidly rising pool. These people, who we might call "the poor," live lives that are envied the world over even today by those not fortunate enough to live within our country. It doesn't matter they now have access to a constant stream of food, peaceful sleep, or medical care. It doesn't matter how many people died to ensure these luxuries remained available— there are many who do not have as much as the others, and for those that hate inequality, that simply cannot stand.

As anti-American rhetoric continues to spiral out of control, people are understandably concerned about violent conflict, with frequent mentions of a second Civil War. "Civil" war is an erroneous concept. It implies a conflict of two groups within the same country. While many hate America and all that it stands for, even the concept of nationhood itself has become abhorrent. They would fight not to preserve America, but to destroy it. But even more, they would go to war to prevent anyone from forming *any* nation again—particularly those who built the United States. They innately realize this country wasn't successful because it was built on magic dirt or its founding documents written on magic paper. It was built on a set of ideas that a very specific set of people are capable of creating again and again. And they want to prevent that.

The good news? No matter how the next few years play out, "America" as we remember it can exist again. In all likelihood, it *will* exist again. With the knowledge of what made America successful, it needn't be a fluke, an oddity, or isolated coincidence of clever writing and rich soil. As a concept, America may be inevitable, springing forth whenever and wherever faithful Christians decide to direct themselves with an acknowledgement of personal liberty, limited government, and the constant outward- and upward-facing thanks and praise to the author of all order. Not equality, but order. Life, liberty, and pursuit of happiness weren't inevitable results of human progress but miraculously happened despite it. With careful instruction and prayer, they can be ours again.

Introspection

As our nation and the churches sprinkled throughout continue their fall away from God, you may find yourself starting to ask questions about the future: Will I be able to worship in peace? Will I be able to live in peace? Will my children? Will they have a stable country in which they can grow up and have their own families, free from violence, civil unrest, and religious persecution? If you haven't begun to ask these questions yet, you should.

I couldn't imagine twenty years ago that I would seriously be considering these topics, but it has become clear that things are accelerating downwards. California's governor recently signed new legislation that reduced punishments for adults that have sex with minors. Public parades across our nation openly celebrate sodomy and other perversions unfit to speak of. Women dance and sing songs in celebration of the abortion of thousands of unborn children. Children are stripped away from their parents and forcefully injected with vaccines that can cause debilitating neurological and autoimmune conditions.

Corporate and government employees are made to apologize for their skin color in public "struggle sessions" designed to intimidate and humiliate. The University of Rhode Island recently decided to remove two murals which honored veterans from World War II because the soldiers depicted were mostly white—an accurate historical representation. As a result, our military veterans are being scorned, even attacked, simply for having served their country.

Law and order is disappearing before our eyes. Police are mocked and ridiculed by those they risk their lives to protect. Foreigners freely enter our country with little respect for our nation's laws or customs and receive generous benefits as their reward. And our nation's flag is considered too controversial by some homeowner's associations to even be displayed—a pronouncement far more humiliating than any banner-burning protest.

Financially, we are living on borrowed time. Many people live on non-existent money, lent to them by corporations whose stock market values are conjured from thin air. Material excess is preached from the pulpit every Sunday and the usury which feeds it is not even mentioned. Everywhere you look, no matter where you look, our descent into irresponsibility and wickedness are there. It is quickly becoming impossible to avoid the foreboding sense that the stability and security of our once-great Christian nation are disappearing.

Human nature dictates that we look away. Most people prefer to paper over signs of deterioration by learning to avoid these things. We steer clear of certain websites or accounts on the internet. We talk about happy things at church and with our families. We study the scriptures intently—anything to ignore the enemy plotting at our gates.

But those questions I mentioned earlier will begin to haunt, for we have no answers. *Will I be able to worship in peace?* Politicians are already openly advocating financial attacks for those churches who don't affirm LGBTQ agendas. As fewer true Christian churches remain, they may begin to feel more comfortable meeting in secret. *Will I be able to live in peace?* People are already being physically attacked for their political views, their ability to speak freely—even for the color of their skin. The news will not cover these stories, but for those who take the time to look, violence is upon us already.

Will my children inherit a stable country in which they can get married and start their own families, free from violence, civil unrest, and religious persecution? You would be crazy to believe our country is trending towards a more cohesive, civil society with less violence. We are obviously not—each day brings seemingly more uncivil behavior from increasingly unstable people. A massive violent outburst feels just a spark away from ignition.

As I struggled to answer these questions myself, I began to feel that something significant was needed—a radical departure from simply a desire for more fervent prayer or scriptural study. To form a new church—an ambitious project in and of itself—seemed like the wrong approach. Everyone has their doctrinal differences, for sure, but the issues plaguing us today are not really theological in nature. The same could apply towards the formation of a new denomination—the remedy for the darkness that surrounds us will not be found in the perfect set of bylaws or belief statements. We have a much larger issue to deal with, one which even a specific denominational response cannot encompass.

Even a nationwide call for revival is unlikely to effect meaningful change—many Christians themselves are unwittingly endorsing the very ideological concepts that are destroying us, confident this is precisely what God wants. Their worship of equality above all things has turned them against those who seek to embrace God's natural order and the political freedom and security which descends from it. Through our Creator, all things are possible—I believe that whole heartedly—but a thorough survey of the political and religious landscapes have convinced me that America as we once knew may be over. Something else may need to be done.

Future

When the Amish began to leave for America in the 1700s, it was a desperate time. Centuries of wars that featured Christians torturing and killing each other had taken their toll. The journey was expensive, perilous, and promised little beyond a sliver of hope for a less violent chance at survival. America was a faraway place where a brutal existence against the elements awaited them—a striking indicator of the fear they had for their Christian brethren.

Can *we* make it? Will *we* survive? Much of this depends on our ability to navigate the muddy waters of equality. Can we accept inequality not as the inevitable result of a fallen world, but the perfect design of an intricate machine whose rattle and hum we cannot perfectly comprehend? The ability to answer yes to that question, I'm afraid, will be very difficult for even devoted followers of Jesus— something the Tree of Knowledge has destined us to rebel against. As our nation and churches continue their descent into madness, professing anything other than universal equality will likely become a perilous testimony.

If you can answer *yes*—if after reading this book or reconsidering the natural order of creation, if after intense prayer and discussion—if you can accept that inequality *is* an essential, intentional component of God's lavish design, and that the rejection of it has and will lead to misery and destruction, then I think we will find it very easy to like each other. You and I, and others who agree on this, will have the foundation for a very tight-knit group of believers that are likely to agree on many other important things—a much needed respite from the discord we currently face every day.

The original concept of America isn't just a clear and present danger to those who worship equality—its *re-creation* is a future danger so long as Christians are brave enough to proclaim God's truth and celebrate the order present throughout his creation. America, as it was originally conceived, is failing not because it has rebelled against capitalism or limited government or personal liberty, but because it has rebelled against God himself. We cannot save our country by "reaching across the aisle" and trying to achieve political compromise, for the enemy are directly amongst us, in our same political parties and sitting beside us at church. Our detractors do not want a left-leaning America—they would prefer that America not exist at all and would instead become a beacon of equality and sameness the rest of the world's countries would dissolve within. The notion that God would favor a group of people who honored his commands with a peaceful and prosperous nation—they'd be ecstatic to see that relegated to the dustbin of history.

As a result, we can—and should—pray for revival across this country. With a massive rebirth of Christianity and new appreciation for creation's natural order, America as it once was might spark to life once again. But as someone who is neither pacifist nor fatalist, I must ask how we—as like-minded Christians—can move forward to both advance the Kingdom and secure a future for our existence?

Unlike the Amish, there is no unexplored territory we can now escape to. Beside the frozen tundras of Antarctica, nations have expanded their borders to encapsulate nearly every available acre of earth. To add to the problem, over the last hundred years advances in international travel and the unwillingness to enforce immigration law have set the hook on a grand experiment in multiculturalism, a knot of disparate languages, cultures, traditions, and religions that will be very difficult to untangle.

Even believers are falling away from the faith every day as their congregations and pastors offer them no meaningful alternative to the equality-driven peace and unity promised to them outside—and indeed, inside—the church. Additionally, they are offered no protection or instruction in how to handle the attacks of bigotry leveled against them and many succumb to the outrage of the mob rather than try and defend themselves.

We cannot assume that revival will be the course of events and so with no destination to direct our pilgrimage, we, as Christians, must begin to defend Christendom. Because of these things, and in order to preserve—or possibly create—a thriving Christian community, there are several initiatives we must focus our efforts on:

1. We must teach the Bible, the sinfulness of mankind, and the desire for God's redemption through Jesus Christ alone.

2. We must teach and instruct children and adults to recognize and celebrate the beauty of God's creation and the wonder of his natural order. Men & Women. Family & Church. Nations & Creation.

3. We must teach and instruct everyone in the value of personal liberty, limited government, capitalism, and the freedom to express a plurality of Christian faiths.

4. We must teach believers to recognize and refute modern heresies growing like cancer within their congregations: equality, social justice, and critical race theory.

5. We must remind adults and children of the poverty and despair humanity lived through under monarchal and dictatorial rule. We must teach and remind them of the incredible gift America provided.

6. We must prepare for the possibility of a difficult future. We must prepare for the chance we will have to defend our commitment to our faith through geographical clustering, financial partnerships, and possibly violent conflict.

7. We must disavow all violence for the sake of personal gain or enforcing these views on others. Similarly, we must disavow all pacifism in our efforts to defend these beliefs for ourselves from those who would encroach upon them.

If you have never considered the future that may await committed Christians, these may seem like drastic measures. As someone who has studied the rise and fall of great nations, I can assure you, they are not. The time for inaction has long passed us. We can no longer hide within our plush sanctuaries on Sunday mornings, hoping the mobs of those who hate us pass us over. Their numbers—and boldness—increase each day. We must reach out to like-minded Christians beyond the confines of our church or denomination and lash ourselves together around these seven points and by so doing, form new kinships that will survive the coming storm.

How might we enact these things?

1. By encouraging churches across the country to adopt this resolution by committing to the teaching and instruction of the seven topics mentioned above.

2. By the creation of training materials, videos, books, conferences, and homeschool curriculums that prepare Christians to defend their faith and nationhood.

3. By the creation of para-church organizations which work across congregations and denominations to instruct and guide men, women and children in the fostering of these ideals.

Although we may one day have a distinct garb or language that draw us together, for now it is enough to look towards a land, a nation, where Christians who believe in inequality as a natural feature of God's great design may live and love in peace. I urge to you pray for these same things.

If you are interested in following its progress—or want to get involved—I have already started discussing one such community. I can make no guarantees it will actually happen, but you can follow along on My Incredible Opinion (www.myincredibleopinion.com), where I talk about all of these things. The Amish 2.0, I often call it. Hopefully, there will be many others.

Other popular books by Forrest Maready:

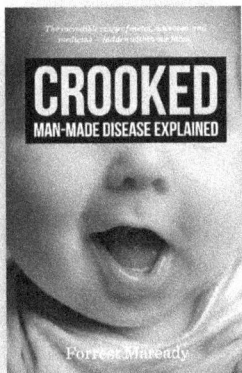

Crooked:
The incredible story of metal, microbes,
and medicine—hidden with our faces.

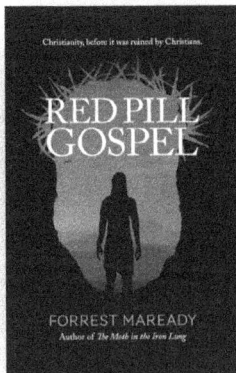

Red Pill Gospel
Christianity, before it was
ruined by Christians.

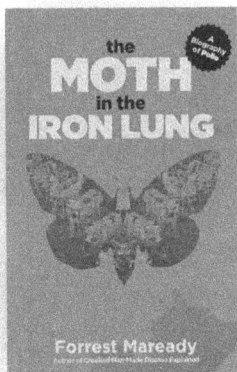

The Moth in the Iron Lung:
The story of polio that
explains everything.

Unvaccinated:
Why parents are choosing
natural immunity.

CPSIA information can be obtained
at www.ICGtesting.com
Printed in the USA
LVHW112002280223
740570LV00003B/318